'This wonderful book transcends its genre by being simultaneously compelling and graceful – in the fullest sense of those words.

'Visionary but grounded, inspiring but practical, it brims with the writers' joy at their journeys and their utter confidence that equal joy is already in the grasp of any reader who cares to walk alongside them in this celebration of life, spirit and growth.

'It captures every smile and heartbeat of Susannah and Ya'Acov's real-life teaching, and – like all great wisdom – revels in paradox: its most powerful insights are those it presents with the lightest touch.

Above all, this book is deeply, compassionately human – vivid, timeless and universal. It rings with quiet truth and is a delight to read.'

George Tiffin – TV drama and feature film writer

'Ya'Acov & Susannah Darling Khan are pointing out a direction, outlining a way for every human being to discover and unfold the essence of their movement tendencies. Guided by their visions and dreams, they describe archetypal forces emerging and combining into a flow in their movement medicine. Try it!'

Arny and Amy Mindell – authors of *Quantum Mind and Healing*

'Ya'Acov and Susannah have through many years of practice and exploration opened up a path of self-empowerment and healing, through combining old earth-based teachings with contemporary movement practice in their own unique way. They are pathfinders and renewers, who dance their talk, and their excitement for sharing their discoveries shines through this book.'

Chris Luttichau – author of *Animal Spirit Guides*, founder and teacher of Northern Drum Shamanic Centre

'This book is both a wonderful introduction to Ya'Acov and Susannah's collective life experiences so far and a fabulous instruction manual for the next stage. It is also wonderful set of menu options for the soul, full of tangy dishes and clashing flavours and the invitation to try something different. I particularly love the juxtaposition of insight with personal experience – because it takes us right into the authors' own journey – there's nothing like the wisdom of fellow travellers to light up the way.'

Nicholas McInery – dramatist and screenwriter

'Ya'acov and Susannah are inspirational and profound teachers who live, breathe and walk this path. This book is a distillation of many years of study and practice. I know of no one more qualified, or able, to teach movement as a spiritual journey.'

Malcolm Stern – psychotherapist, author, TV presenter and co-founder of Alternatives at St James' Church, Piccadilly, London

'Movement medicine taps the intrinsic dynamism in each of us. The impulse toward wholeness is indeed part our miraculous nature, and this book is an elegant cue toward the wonders awaiting us. We may discover the human being and the cosmos are synonymous. We may learn we are not only entitled to this great freedom, but designed for it. *Movement Medicine* is a must-read for mortals.'

Stuart Davis – writer, director and songwriter

'Ya'Acov and Susannah are seasoned explorers of the psyche, who have built up a fantastic and well-deserved reputation over the years and this profound body of work represents the fruits of a lifetime's devotion. Not just a flash-in-the-pan change-your-life-in-seven-days pretender, this book is a solid contribution to the human experiment that can serve as a stalwart companion and transformational tool for the rest of your life.'

Barefoot Doctor

'It's great. Useful, practical and inspiring. This is a book that generously offers a wealth of combined experience and practical exercises. It is for all who love to move and dance and for all who seek fulfillment and expansion on this life path home to ourselves. It has so much to offer and can be dipped into or read from cover to cover. It combines depth with light heartedness and honesty with compassion. It offers a particular path and discipline that can be as rigorous or as free as you choose.'

Sue Kuhn – psychotherapist and accredited 5 Rhythms teacher

'If you want to dance your way to God, to experience yourself liberated in body, heart and soul, then *Movement Medicine* is an essential orientation. The Darling Khans, who write with zest and love, rightly say, "Once we enter the flow of our own movement we learn to trust the natural creativity of the life force inside us." We, as explorers in the sphere of human sexuality, find *Movement Medicine* to be real treasure. Consciously rooted in the body and embracing the power of elemental forces, the reader is invited into 9 Gateways of experience through which lie healing, empowerment and transformation. *Movement Medicine* represents a great call to our awakening with the reminder that "the spirit of the dance is waiting for you"!'

Puja Richardson – author of *The Love Keys*

'This book reminded me of an experience with Ya'Acov, who was leading a workshop at the Society for Shamanic Practitioners Conference in 2008, when 100 people were dancing as one; I again felt that experience of having my inner dancer opened up and once more felt myself dancing within a community. Wonderful.'

Elsa Malpas – Society of Shamanic Practitioners

'The recipes are not only great to read, but they really work. The personal stories are a delight. This book is another reminder of how good it feels to love oneself.'

Howard Malpas – Society of Shamanic Practitioners

Movement Medicine
How to Awaken, Dance
and Live your Dreams

Movement Medicine
How to Awaken, Dance and Live your Dreams

Susannah & Ya'Acov Darling Khan

HAY HOUSE

Australia • Canada • Hong Kong • India
South Africa • United Kingdom • United States

First published and distributed in the United Kingdom by:
Hay House UK Ltd, 292B Kensal Rd, London W10 5BE. Tel.: (44) 20 8962
1230; Fax: (44) 20 8962 1239. www.hayhouse.co.uk

Published and distributed in the United States of America by:
Hay House, Inc., PO Box 5100, Carlsbad, CA 92018-5100. Tel.: (1) 760
431 7695 or (800) 654 5126; Fax: (1) 760 431 6948 or (800) 650 5115.
www.hayhouse.com

Published and distributed in Australia by:
Hay House Australia Ltd, 18/36 Ralph St, Alexandria NSW 2015. Tel.: (61)
2 9669 4299; Fax: (61) 2 9669 4144. www.hayhouse.com.au

Published and distributed in the Republic of South Africa by:
Hay House SA (Pty), Ltd, PO Box 990, Witkoppen 2068. Tel./Fax: (27) 11
467 8904. www.hayhouse.co.za

Published and distributed in India by:
Hay House Publishers India, Muskaan Complex, Plot No.3, B-2, Vasant
Kunj, New Delhi – 110 070. Tel.: (91) 11 4176 1620; Fax: (91) 11 4176
1630. www.hayhouse.co.in

Distributed in Canada by:
Raincoast, 9050 Shaughnessy St, Vancouver, BC V6P 6E5. Tel.: (1) 604
323 7100; Fax: (1) 604 323 2600

© Susannah and Ya'Acov Darling Khan, 2009

The moral rights of the authors have been asserted.

The authors of this book do not dispense medical advice or prescribe
the use of any technique as a form of treatment for physical or medical
problems without the advice of a physician, either directly or indirectly.
The intent of the authors is only to offer information of a general nature
to help you in your quest for emotional and spiritual wellbeing. In the
event you use any of the information in this book for yourself, which
is your constitutional right, the authors and the publisher assume no
responsibility for your actions.

A catalogue record for this book is available from the British Library.

Internal artworks © Matt Marmot of Inner State D-Zines

ISBN 978-1-84850-144-7

Printed in the UK by
CPI William Clowes Ltd,
Beccles, NR34 7TL.

*To the spirit of the dance,
to the magnificence of life on Earth
and to the happiness, peace and liberation
of all beings.*

Contents

In Thanks

Our deepest gratitude to the many people who have supported us on our journeys over the years.

Bee Quick was the first one to support us in our work, swiftly followed by Susanne Perks. Without these two grandmas, we might never have begun. Roland Wilkinson and Susanne Fehr's ongoing support and work over many years have been central to the co-creation of our school. Without you, our dreams would remain up in the air. To our team of dedicated and delightfully crazy organizers, the same goes for you too. And to Rosie and Frazer for your friendship over the years and the best design and travel service on the planet. In the beginning, without Malcolm Barradell and Derek Finch we simply would not have managed. Nor would we have managed without Vicki Latchem's tender care and support over the years. Dancing bodies need good food and we have had the blessing of having Carrie Allcott cook for our groups for more than 15 years.

God knows where we would have ended up without our teachers. In order of appearance in our lives: Ursula Fawcett, Peggy Sherno, John Leary-Joyce, Joseph Zinker, Manas Marmara, Batty Thunder Bear, Donna Talking Leaves, Rose Thunder Eagle, Heather Campbell, Sue Jamieson, Arwyn Dreamwalker, Gabrielle Roth, in the cauldron of whose work our own work evolved over an 18-year apprenticeship, Bikko Matthe Penta, Helen Poyner, Suprapto Suryodamo, Victor Sanchez, Merrilyn Tunneshende, Chloë Goodchild, Sandra Smith, Julian Marshall, Carioca, Adrian Freedman, Hamilton Souther and Alberto Torres Davila, Kajuyali Tsamani, Vivian Broughton, Albrecht Mahr and the spirit of the forest. Our thanks come from our hearts.

We're blessed by the best bunch of friends any pair of dancing lunatics could hope for. Special thanks for your support with the process of writing this book to: David Rose and Julie Deal, Jake and Eva Chapman, Julie Devine, Sue Kuhn, Susie and Iwan Kushka, Benjamin Schiess, Jo Hardy, Matthew Barley and Vika Mullova, Joseph Serra and Elizabeth Josephs-Serra, Volker Kaczinski, Mati Engwerda and Saryo Van Lakerfeld, Sarah Patterson, Chris Luttichau and the Wenzls.

A big thank you to our fellow teachers and friends who have been such excellent companions in the long-time dance: Alain Allard and Sarah Pitchford, Andrew Holmes, Bernadette Ryder, Caroline Carey, Cathy Ryan, Chloë and Christian de Sousa, Dawn Morgan, Dilys Morgan-Scott, Hege Gabrielsen, Mark Boylan and Sarah Blagg, Sue Rickards. Once again, there are many more. And special thanks to Kathy Altman, Lori Salzburg and Andrea Juhan for listening and colleagueship over many years.

For your support with the development of Movement Medicine and this book, gratitude to: Michelle Pilley, for your belief in this project and your passion about our world, all the excellent team at Hay House, our skilful and humorous editor Lizzie Hutchins, Chris Odle for your star gazing and support, Sue Law for your deep understanding and feedback and Nick Daws for the great CD about book writing.

Deep gratitude to all our students, past, present and future. It is with you that we have learned and grown, and with you that this work has evolved and will continue to do so.

Love and thanks to our ancestors for handing us the torch so intact and to our dear families for loving us all the way, especially our parents, Elizabeth, Angela, Brian and Richard. And we bow to each other and all the love, sweat and years of which this book is a result. And finally, to our son, who is simply so himself, which, given that he's had to grow up around us, is quite an achievement! Thank you.

Ya'Acov & Susannah Darling Khan, April 2009

Introduction

'The personal life deeply lived always expands into truths beyond itself.'

Anaïs Nin

Movement Medicine is a movement meditation system designed to awaken and connect you to your full potential. It will encourage the seeds that lie as possibilities in the soil of your soul to germinate and flourish into powerful offerings. Do you want to discover the joy of contributing all that you are in your work, your relationships and your world? Do you want to discover the wisdom, freedom and vision of the dancer inside you, whether you are a professional groover or think you have 'two left feet'? Welcome to Movement Medicine.

At this time of great change, we all have the power and the responsibility to wake up and respond to the individual, societal and global challenges before us. The litany of horror that faces us every time we turn on the news is a terrifying mirror of what we are as humans. We have a great capacity to harm:

ourselves, each other and the other creatures of this Earth. We also have an enormous capacity for love, forgiveness, creativity, mercy, transformation and healing. Indeed, these qualities are being expressed all the time, all over the world, but rarely make the news. Yet they can have a great effect. It is all of our zillions of individual choices that determine the quality of life and environment we live in. Imagine the transformative power if each of us were able to discover our purpose and unleash our passion and creativity, embodying the unique gifts and perspectives of our experience and talents. Who's to say it can't happen? All it needs is for each of us to become empowered. And that means taking responsibility for the power we each have to affect our world. We need to ask the question: 'Who am I and what am I here to contribute?' And we need to expand our awareness beyond our own noses, beyond the limits of our own perspectives and self-interest. Now is the time. We have collectively created a situation on this planet where the imperative to wake up is compelling. It is no longer a matter of being alternative. It is a matter of there being *no* alternative.

The good news is that waking up is the best ride in the fair. It's a moving, exciting and unpredictable adventure. There are many routes you can take. Our way is through the 9 Gateways of Movement Medicine.

We have found that an attitude of appreciation and gratitude opens doorways of adventure, possibility and the ordinary ecstasy of waking up with a smile, ready to create on the empty canvas of a new day. Participating in the ongoing evolution of life on Earth is a fast track to fulfilment and satisfaction. Would you like to die with a contented smile on your face, knowing that you'd done what you came here to do? So would we! As the old Zen teaching goes, we wish to burn all the wood we've been given, so that when we are done, these flames will have burned as brightly as they can and we will leave behind no regrets, just ashes and the simple contentment of a life fully lived.

An Archetypal Journey

This work is not a quick fix. The journey we are inviting you to take is lifelong. We can guarantee that there will be joy, inspiration and tears along the way. On the Movement Medicine path, we each need to experience the Divine Yin and the Divine Yang within and the dynamic and creative force that comes from the relationship between them. This relationship gives rise to our creative potential and to the wisdom of the Sage. These archetypal forces arise naturally as we surrender to the spirit of the dance. So we cannot promise that life will become easier, but we can tell you that there is wisdom within you that has taken millions of years to evolve and that the dancer inside you has access to it and can lead you on your way.

We, too, are on our own journeys and we've woven many of our personal stories into this book. They illuminate both the courage and the sense of humour that voyagers on this path may require. They are stories about love, sex, relationship, family, work, death, friendship and the spirit. We share with you the ways we've messed up as well as the ways we've succeeded. We have learned equally from both. Maybe you'll recognize yourself in some of our adventures, laugh with us at our foolishness and smile with recognition at our moments of inspiration. We hope you, too, will find the inspiration to bring more love, movement and joy into your life.

You are standing before a doorway. Should you go through? Anything could happen. Your life could change. You could actually become the person you were supposed to be. And, best of all, you might have to get up and dance.

Why Dance?

'Dance?' we hear you say. 'How's that going to help with my problems? How is dancing going to help me get where I want to in life?' Good questions!

We dance because it brings us untold aliveness and joy. We've learned how to get high on the dance itself. What we discover in that state is potent, personal, and has changed our lives again and again. Dance connects us – with our bodies, with our souls, with each other, with the space within and around us and with the spirit of life. It gives us breathing space away from the noise of our busyness. In that space we come into deeper alignment with ourselves and our own intuitive knowledge. The answers to our inner dilemmas often simply drop into place. Movement Medicine quietens our minds and shifts our attention to the realm of possibility.

Once we enter the flow of our own movement we learn to trust the natural creativity of the life force inside us. Our patterns come to light and by becoming conscious of them we can begin to explore new possibilities. Through our dance practice, these possibilities become literally embodied and rooted in our physicality and thus we cannot help but carry them into the rest of our lives. The life of the dance starts to inform the dance of our life.

Why is Movement Medicine?

On the most basic level, movement is life. The movement of our lungs, of our heart, of our blood keeps us alive. Without movement we are dead. Simple. Without enough movement we stagnate, just as a blocked river stagnates. When we move, we cleanse, invigorate and renew ourselves, just as a moving river cleanses, invigorates and renews itself. Our bodies, our hearts and our minds are designed to move, just as the seasons turn, day becomes night and the moon and tides follow their rhythms. All of life moves. When *we* move, physically, emotionally, mentally, we resonate with life. When we move with consciousness, with our bodies, hearts and minds connected, we nourish the soul and connect with the spirit of life.

Life is a creative, dynamic interplay between stability and change, limits and growth, awareness of what is and movement towards what can be. Bringing consciousness to this play between being and becoming is the basis of Movement Medicine.

Maps and the Truth

We live in times where the spiritual void left by the massive increase in materialism, the deterioration of traditional systems of respect and the mass exodus from religious institutions have led to a deep loneliness and hunger. In this gap, the 'new age' has merrily marketed its wares and offered up all kinds of fascinating and fabulous alternatives that offer meaning and connection. As with all market places, there is a wide variety of quality in what is available.

We have journeyed amongst some of the beautiful teachings that have graced the shores of Europe in recent times. We have been blessed to see ourselves, each other, the world and our universe through many different lenses. Each perspective is whole unto itself and we have learned valuable lessons from all of them. We have come to see each of the traditions we have worked with as a beautiful vessel in the great ocean, providing us with a way to navigate the stormy seas as we take the voyage that has only one destination.

On that voyage, maps, our own mandala included, may be beautiful and valuable, but we feel that ultimately the only authority that each of us can trust is our own experience. That's not to say that we cannot be helped, challenged and supported by friends, teachers, students and of course by life itself. But in the end, as Kajuyali, a Colombian shaman whom we have been lucky to meet and work with recently, said to us, 'The only really important thing is that you can look yourself straight in the eye and know that you have lived from your truth and integrity. Have faith in your truth. Follow it with love.'

And so, as we offer you the distillation of our journey so far and hold up our billboard in praise of possibility, we invite you to imagine that on every page you turn there is a watermark that reminds you that this is not *the* truth. It is a map, a mandala, which, like a piece of a jigsaw, is part of a much bigger picture, or field of wisdom. A map is not the same as the actual landscape and you may need to make a few adaptations as you go along. Use what works for you and let the rest go. It's your life!

Where Did the 9 Gateways of Movement Medicine Come From?

We have been intensively involved in many approaches to healing and personal and social transformation for many years. In the eighties we were both involved in non-violent direct action within the peace movement, through which we met in the rose garden of a squat in Stoke Newington, London. Susannah was completing her degree in anthropology and training in Gestalt psychotherapy with the Gestalt Centre, London. Ya'Acov was completing his degree in visual communications in the Midlands and rediscovering the feeling of living close to spirit that he'd had as a child.

During our first years together, we followed an apprenticeship with the Deer Tribe Metis Sun Dance path and since then we have worked with many shamans and medicine people around the world. Ya'Acov studied intensively with Victor Sanchez and Merrilyn Tunneshende, as well as with a traditional shaman from the Sami tradition whom he'd spent 12 years dreaming about before realizing that he was a living human being. Susannah studied devotional voice with Chloë Goodchild, assisting her for two years with her Naked Voice groups, and continues to study long term with Sandra Smith in vocal technique and Julian Marshall in musical theory and songwriting. We're the lifelong student types and are both continuing our studies in many fascinating areas.

We met Gabrielle Roth in 1988, fell in love with her, her 5 Rhythms™ work, her deep philosophy married with the passionate grace of her dance work and the simple congruency and coherence of her maps. In 1989 we trained with her and became teachers of the 5 Rhythms, introducing it to many countries in Europe. Between 1996 and 2006 we ran the Moving Centre School, UK, representing Gabrielle and the 5 Rhythms work in Europe. The 5 Rhythms maps have been central to our own inner work and understanding and our 18-year apprenticeship with Gabrielle was the cauldron in which our own work evolved. In 2006, we all knew it was time for us to 'leave home', spread our wings and fly.

A key part of our personal movement practice is our ongoing individual work with Helen Poyner, with whom we have been studying both individually and as a couple since 1991. Helen's lineage includes Suprapto Suryodamo and Anna Halprin. We have been deeply helped by her truthful and compassionate mirroring and guiding. She has been and remains an invaluable teacher and companion.

And then in 2005 we found ourselves in Peru, apprenticed to two very wonderful Amazonian shamans whose work humbled and strengthened us both in different and personal ways and enabled us to take our next steps.

Susannah: *The name 'Movement Medicine' came to me one night in a dream in 2002. A deep, strong, clear, resonant voice spoke to me. It said: 'Your work is to be called Movement Medicine.' That was it. I knew it was true. That dream had a presence that stayed with me.*

In Peru, I saw and experienced the healers as columns of light, grounded in the earth and rising to the stars. I saw how I needed to stand up, both physically and metaphorically. I understood the importance of aligning with the vertical axis, and how in much of my former work I had been preoccupied with the horizontal phenomenological world of experience and relationship. This sounds rather abstract, but it has transformed my life and teaching. It means paying attention to my primary relationship with spirit. It means standing up tall with humility and strength, connected with Earth and sky. It means standing in my own sense of integrity and doing the work to make action congruent with intention. This has meant offloading some old baggage. As I've done the work of opening my 'shame closets' to the light of healing, I have lost the fear of being seen. In the process, I have realized that there is nothing I can hide from spirit anyway. Then the horizontal world of relationship and experience can orientate around this vertical axis.

This has become a central part of our movement practice and is reflected in our mandala as the Tree of Life. The 5 bottom circles point to the roots and the 9 Gateways map the branches. Long ago, when I left medical school, a friend joked that she could see me as a wildly creative and eccentric drama teacher having all the students play at being trees. She was right!

Ya'Acov: *One night in the summer of 2005 we were sitting in a ceremony in the heart of the Peruvian Amazon. It was the dark of the moon and yet even then the forest seemed to glow from a deep and primal source at its roots. We were there as a family. It had taken a 12-hour flight to Lima, a two-hour flight over the Andes to Iquitos, a 15-hour boat journey up the Amazon to Genaro Herrera and then an eight-hour canoe journey down an almost dried-out tributary to get there. The rains had been sparse and with the canoes loaded down with supplies for 15 people for 10 days, there were times when we had to get out and push. Our fears about piranhas disappeared as we watched the others happily leap barelegged into the mud and realized* that our help was really needed! The Amazonian mud swallowed our weight as we heaved the canoes through the narrow canals. There was a moment when I was sitting at the prow in just my Calvin Klein briefs, legs darkened by the mud, looking at my son at the other end of the canoe as the rain fell, when I had to laugh. Some moments in life are just surreal and memorable. We call them 'pearl moments'. That was one of them!

A few days later we were in the ceremony in the heart of the jungle. The gentle and insistent leafy sound of the shaman's shakapa (leaf rattle) and icaros (spirit songs) was hypnotic and the night-time melodies of the forest were all part of the symphony. I was deeply in trance. And then I saw our mandala above and in front of me, suspended in the air, spinning beautifully. I had originally seen it in a dream and had worked with an artist to get it just right. We knew that it contained new teachings and wisdom for us. And now here I was in the Amazon, being flattened by a torrent of primal patterns and energies rushing at me in a vision so strong that I struggled to maintain any consciousness at all.

The shaman told me to stand up as the vision came towards me. I saw a perfect tapestry of trees and animal spirits, jaguars, anacondas, hummingbirds and eagles, all blending in with beings that I had never seen anywhere before. I struggled to stand. I truly felt that I was going to be steamrollered by this surge of primal rainforest energy, but it all stopped right in front of me.

I didn't know it, but I had come to an interview. 'Why was I here? Did I want to learn? If so, what?'

I answered the questions as directly as I could and I felt that my answers were heard. If I had known what I was beginning at that moment, I truly do not know if I would have had the strength or the courage to communicate so directly. But I said that I did want to learn – I wanted *to learn to embody a balance between personal power and humility. The process of being humbled took months and, in all honesty, wasn't a pretty sight. In fact it was a massacre.*

After I'd answered my questioners, the vision cleared, to be replaced by a very clear image of our mandala. It shone in the space, moving beautifully and appearing full of mystery. I looked at it and a voice above and behind me told me, 'Ya'Acov, there are 9 gateways to the soul. Your mandala is a map. Learn to read it.'

That was it. Clear and simple and then it was gone.

And that was the beginning of a process that has been the culmination of years of study.

Since then we have been engaged in a fascinating progression of learning to read the map we were given. In prayer, meditation, many ceremonies and much chewing over the material we have been gathering over the years, we have distilled the essence of what we received. In the practice of teaching we have found working with this mandala to be effective and potent.

Back in Peru a year later, we were given the next chapter and guided to a new level of understanding. This book is the story of what has been revealed so far. We're writing it because we feel so ridiculously blessed that we just had to share it with you. We have travelled with some remarkable people and have been blessed to have had many extraordinary and totally dedicated teachers on the way. We will always be grateful to Gabrielle Roth, who was our central teacher for so many years. She was the one who saw the potential locked inside us and gave us the means to access it.

Each of our teachers has influenced us and each of them is present in both who we are and what we are sharing with you. We long ago let go of the myth of independence in favour of the reality of interdependence. If you look at the maps that we have synthesized, you will see the ancient and the modern, the psychotherapeutic and the shamanic, the devotional and the traditional, the scientific and the mystical, all woven together into material that has proven strong enough to make sails to take our ship through the stormy seas. We exist in a continuum of evolution that makes this fusion of forms and ideas inevitable.

The dance has found its way into every area of our lives. It empowers us and deepens our connection to the people we are with and the environment we are in. This is the gift of a body-based spiritual practice. It returns us to the actual present-time sensory experience in which we are connected. There are days when the dance floor seems to have expanded to include the high street, the kitchen floor, the garden, the bedroom and even the office, and everything truly is a dance.

How to Use This Book

Please feel free to read through the book in order or to dance around the pages and go wherever your interest takes you. Though our work is precise, it is not linear.

We have discovered time and time again that the major difference between great dreams that go up in a puff of smoke and great dreams that come into being is one simple thing: *action*. This book is a call to *action*.

One of Ya'Acov's teachers was a man called Victor Sanchez. Like many thousands of people, he read the books of Carlos Castaneda, an anthropology student of South American sorcery. Like many thousands of people, he talked with his friends about whether the things that Castaneda wrote about were possible. Unlike many others, he then put his thoughts into action. He gathered a group of his friends and meticulously set to work to examine the concepts that Castaneda was sharing by mimicking the practices that Castaneda's teachers gave to him. Needless to say, he had a lot of very fascinating experiences! So our suggestion to you is to try out the 'recipes' we offer throughout the book and find out for yourself whether Movement Medicine has any practical value in your life.

Anybody in a body can do this. So that means you. Take a deep breath. Your drum is calling you. Its rhythm is in your blood. To those of you who love to dance and those who never have, to those of you who used to dance and stopped, to those of you who believe you have two left feet, whoever you are, wherever you've come from, however old you are and whatever you look like, the spirit of the dance is waiting for you. Go ahead, take a chance, wiggle your toes, dance!

.•.• Part I •.•.

The Dance of Creation

Chapter 1
Dancing at the Centre of your own Circle

'The original Tao gives rise to the One
The One gives rise to the Two,
The Two gives rise to the Three,
The Three gives rise to the ten thousand things.'

Tao Te Ching

At the very centre of everything is the still point, the silence, the void and the emptiness from which all manifestation arises and to which it returns. It is the place of all potential. It is spirit, it is the Tao, it is the thousand other names we have for the ineffable divine presence that creates life and the universe.

One step out from the centre and we enter the eternal dance of polarity, the dance between yin and yang, being and doing, receptivity and action, dark and light, Earth and sky, acceptance and intention. It is the force of attraction between opposites that creates the conditions for the actualization of life in this universe. For us, this force is divine love.

Yin & Yang

The basis of Movement Medicine practice rests in the creative meeting of yin and yang energy from which everything is born, whether it is the universe we live in or the person we are. We have found that awareness of the relationship between our inner yang and inner yin energies is the key to becoming a conscious co-creator in life.

The dance of creation didn't, as the great book likes to tell us, take place in seven days and then stop. It started somewhere and somehow, and has never stopped since. Before breakfast today and every day, the force of creation continued its merry expression through the great mystery of time and space and evolved in a million manifestations. You are one of them.

From the moment of your conception, you have been shaped by an interplay of yin and yang energies and patterns from your parents, your ancestors, the culture you grew up in and your own ways of being and doing. As long as you remain unconscious of these energies and patterns, you are destined to repeat them. Some of this inheritance will have been forged from generations of wisdom and will serve you well throughout your life. Other stories, beliefs and ways of being will not serve you at all. On the contrary, without conscious intervention, they will lead you in a kind of repetitive *déjà vu* sleepwalk down dead-end streets. Movement Medicine practice is a way to work with these forces and become a conscious and empowered participant in the ongoing adventure of creation.

Note: **Though we are not Taoists we have taken the liberty of borrowing the words 'yin' and 'yang' to describe the complementary polarities of creation. Yin and yang are free of the gender associations and confusions that make using 'feminine' and 'masculine' such a minefield.**

The Movement Medicine Mandala

In the four directions (north, south, east and west) of the Movement Medicine mandala are the elemental powers of creation: earth, fire, water and wind. In the centre is the dance of polarities, including the one between yin and yang, represented by the Tree of Life and the Phoenix which rests in its branches. Dancing at the centre of your own circle means being aware of all these forces and getting to know how to work with them.

The Tree of Life
The Tree of Life simultaneously grows down, rooting deep into the dark earth, and grows up, towards the light, into the heavens. It is the perfect symbol of communion between the physical Earth world and the spiritual heights.

The Phoenix
The Phoenix is at the centre of our mandala because we believe passionately in the transformative power of life, specifically the life force within each of us. It reminds us that everything is part of the transformative cycle of death and rebirth and the great cycle of existence through which everything moves.

To us, the Great Mystery of Life is a dance. Every one of us has a dancer inside us and this dancer is more than capable of dancing with whatever life, or what we like to call 'the Great Choreographer', brings us. When we learn to dance with the forces of creation that are present within us, we become conscious of the power we have to effect change and to co-create with life on a personal, relational and environmental level.

Being the Tree of Life

When we first began teaching movement as spiritual practice and were getting into our nomadic lifestyle, we would often find ourselves on trains and planes having rather tricky conversations about the exact nature of our work. We were passionate about the experiences we were having and sharing with others in our workshops, but it took many years to be able to articulate them in a way that people could understand.

At first the conversations went something like this: 'It's dance, but it's meditation. Well, shamanic really. What's shamanic? Oh, you know, ecstatic, trance, journeys in the inner world kind of thing...'

'Mmmm, yes, I see. Like when you pretend to be trees. Is that what you mean?'

Not wanting to be thought of as inconsequential new age hippies, we would respond: 'No, no, it's much deeper than that...'

We were horrified that people might think we were playing at being trees, but now, 20 years on, we realize that they were right. What better metaphor is there than dancing like trees? Deep roots, strong and fluid trunk and branches that reach way up to the celestial realms? Yes, that's about right. A healthy tree is a picture of balance. The deeper the roots go into the earth, the more it can grow towards the light. It dances with the seasons, joyfully sharing its blossom and fruit and giving a magnificent display of colour and life as the autumn comes and strips it naked for the winter.

The beginning of this first meditation on our journey together is adapted from a meditation we learned from a wonderful yoga teacher called Gretchen Faust. It's about connecting with the Tree of Life metaphor in a practical way.

The Tree of Life Meditation

- **Intention:** To feel the Tree of Life within you and outside you.

- **Purpose:** To prepare and ground you for the Movement Medicine journey.

You can do this meditation inside or out. Ideally, you'll find a large mature tree, somewhere where you feel safe and won't be disturbed. If the weather is warm enough, stand barefoot in front of your tree. Or you can do this inside where you can visualise a fine tree of life for yourself.

With bare feet, stand relaxed in a balanced, open stance on the ground in front of your tree, be it physical or imaginary.

Settle the mind into the body, breathing and becoming present.

Ask your chosen tree to be your teacher for this process. Listen...

Shift your attention to the roots of your chosen tree companion. Feel how the roots go deep down into the ground and spread out, drawing the living energy of the Earth up into the body of the tree. Then focus on the trunk. Sense the sap in the tree and the life force that gives it its fluidity and strength. Then focus on the branches. Feel how they reach for the nourishment that comes from the light of the sun, how they are washed by the rain and dance in the wind. Feel how this tree unfurls its leaves, its flowers and fruits as the season dictates.

Sense the tree as a being that bridges the Earth and the heavens.

Now, closing your eyes, bring your attention inside. Breathing in, locate your mind in your head. As you breathe out, let your attention travel down through your head and neck until it rests in your shoulders.

Breathe into the mind in the shoulders and, as you breathe out, let your attention sink down through your torso, resting in your hips. Breathing into your attention in your hips, as you breathe out, let your attention drop down through your thighs to rest in your knees. Breathing into your attention in your knees, let your attention travel down through your lower legs until it rests, breathing, in your feet. Through your feet, feel into the connection between the earth of your body and the body of the Earth. Imagine the soles of your feet opening and let your physical weight pour down through your open feet, feeling your own roots rooting down into the Earth.

Breathe through these roots, connecting with the earth energy circuits, acknowledging and thanking the Earth for holding and supporting you and all of life.

See if you can keep this sense of ground and height as you open your eyes and see yourself as a tree amongst many trees in the forest. How grounded do you feel?

Find one gesture or shape that describes the acceptance of what is true and another that describes your intention to further develop your 'tree self' and all that can grow from that.

Find a simple gesture of respect and gratitude for the tree that has been your teacher for this meditation.

Once you have done this once, you can do it again, just visualizing the tree you worked with.

Acceptance and Intention

'Value what you have but seek for more.'

Isocrates, fourth century BC

Acceptance and intention are two important aspects of the dance of the inner yin and yang. When you rest in acceptance of how you are *and* are empowered by your intention to become all you can be, you are saying a big double 'yes' to yourself.

Acceptance

Authentic and deep self-acceptance is like a fire warming a house. It evokes comfort and reassurance and a relaxed pleasure in being which warms all who come into contact with it. As Prapto, an amazing movement meditation teacher we have worked with, often says, 'Relax in your condition.' With this inner relaxation there is no need to hide, to defend or to keep parts of yourself secret. It is the key to fearless self-enquiry.

It also gives you the rootedness to send your intention out into the world. When an archer sends their arrow towards the target, their feet need to be firmly anchored on the ground. The sending of the arrow reflects the power of intention. For this to be effective you must be anchored in reality, have 'your feet on the ground' and be rooted in what is. That gives you the stability to send your arrow of intention, swift and sure and true, to its target.

Unconditional love and acceptance are also linked to archetypal mother energy. Many of us have not been blessed with this gift of unconditional love, but we can develop it as we take the responsibility of becoming the stewards of our own selves.

Loving the Self

Though we exist in a culture which flaunts the self, true self-acceptance and love are rare. For many, the presentation of a carefully manufactured self masks an inner landscape of self-criticism. This is so normal in our culture that we fail to notice it. We take it for granted that it is the way things are.

A friend told us that she had been at a lecture by a Tibetan meditation teacher. When he was answering questions from the floor, one of his replies started with: 'Well, you need to practise loving them in the same way that you love yourself.'

The questioner interrupted: 'But what if you don't love yourself?'

The teacher scratched his head. 'I'm not sure I understand,' he said. 'You're telling me you don't love yourself?'

The questioner nodded.

The teacher paused again, taking this in, pain and astonishment shadowing his face. When he asked how many people in the room recognized this struggle, almost every hand was raised.

Watching this wise and compassionate teacher reeling from the recognition of this cultural wound made a huge impact on our friend. In the mirror of his surprise, she understood that our difficulty with loving ourselves was a disease personal to western culture, not something pandemic to the human condition as a whole.

With some of our intensive groups, we work with video feedback. Two by two, the students are videoed doing their own dance and then together we watch the footage. Each person has a few minutes in the 'hot seat', where the task is to become your own teacher and to witness yourself with love, compassion and truth. This, as you may imagine, can be a challenge! Many people have a strong and unconscious tendency towards self-laceration, which means that to begin with they can only see the negative in themselves. This amounts to having a chronic auto-immune disease on the psychological level. We have witnessed person after person unable to see the beauty, dignity or strength that to everyone else in the room is utterly self-evident. It's as if, when they look at themselves, they become selectively blind. Our role is to support them in becoming conscious of this habitual pattern of self-criticism, which has usually been created as a way of survival. Step by step, the windows of perception can be cleaned so that the person at least gets a glimpse of their beauty. The presence of trusted witnesses is part of what gives this process such tender and poignant power.

Of course, there are also those who only see the bright lights about themselves. But this is surprisingly rare.

Wherever they are coming from, whenever a person starts to treat themselves with even-handed respect, honesty and love, the relief is palpable. Often the whole group is moved to tears.

Once we have a little sanctuary of trust and acceptance in ourselves, the world changes. For those of us who have had to endure stormy seas and have suffered longstanding neglect, hate or cruelty, building this sanctuary is truly a heroic journey.

Accepting who we are also entails accepting what is. When we stop fighting reality, a simplicity and ease appear in our lives. What is, is. Whether we accept it and let it be or accept it and decide to do something to change it, our capacity to see things as they are gives us a sure ground, a ground of being.

Nature is a wonderful teacher both for the acceptance of how things are and the pull to evolve and become all that we can be. Everything arises and falls in its season. And everything is itself.

Intention

Intention is the other side of the coin, balancing the relaxation of acceptance with the archetypal yang attributes of direction, drive and desire. The great author Ursula Le Guin talks about how life becomes boring when we are just 'being' and on the other hand becomes pointless if we are just focused on 'becoming'.

Imagine holding a beautiful glowing acorn in your hand. It would probably never occur to you to criticize it. An acorn is an acorn. At the same time it is not an oak tree. In order to grow into one it has to crack open and let go of being an acorn. At this point it is vulnerable; it could be eaten by a deer or stepped on by a boot. Yet if it is going to become a beautiful oak tree, it has to make this transition. We are the same.

Intention, imagination, dreams, wanting more from life, from ourselves, for ourselves, for others and for the world are all important and natural aspects of being a growing human being. Take a moment to think of all the amazing inventions and seemingly impossible intentions we have witnessed over the past two centuries alone. Whether you think of the use of electricity, the invention of the bicycle or the crumbling of the Berlin Wall, they all happened because someone dared to dream, to imagine something that did not yet exist and to apply themselves to creating it.

Intention gives our psyche a direction and creates an energy field which opens the way for its own realization. Intention plus action is a change-bringer. Intention plus sustained action is a powerful change-bringer. Intention plus sustained action plus gratitude for that which is intended is deep, grounded magic.

As Goethe famously said:

'Until one is committed, there is hesitancy, the chance to draw back ... the moment one definitely commits oneself, then Providence moves too... Whatever you can do, or

dream you can do, begin it. Boldness has genius, power, and magic in it. Begin it now.'

Balance and Imbalance

The dynamic balance and meeting of yin and yang reverberate through every aspect of life, and Movement Medicine is no exception. Just as the first stage of surrender in giving birth is balanced by the active power of pushing in later stages, so it is in life. Accepting ourselves as we are and giving birth to who we can become needs both strong and balanced yin and yang attributes. However, we often over-identify with one or other end of the spectrum.

Over-identification with Yang

When we talk about yang energy, we are talking about active energy and the power of intention, forward movement and evolution. These qualities work beautifully, dynamically and in harmony with the nourishing and accepting force of yin energy.

What happens in an individual or a collective where the yang principle has become unbalanced and lost its connection to the yin? Take a look around – the answers are everywhere to be seen. In our culture, yang energy has become disconnected from the roots, acceptance and knowledge of the cyclical nature of life. It is therefore ungrounded, full of tension and driven in a never-ending spiral of onward and upward achievement. When growth slows down in the economy, as it has done worldwide over these recent difficult times, we hear panicked presenters, politicians and company directors complaining that profit is down for this quarter. But when we look at nature, we see that there are times of growth and times of harvest, times of activity and times of quiet and rest. If we look at the cycle of the year, we see that nature makes use of all the different seasons. For instance, in the winter, when it looks as if very little is growing at all, there is a lot going on deep down in the roots of the trees as they prepare themselves for another cycle of growth. What would happen to a tree that lost touch with this natural cycle and decided that constant growth was the way? It might shoot up very fast in a fine display of yang expression, but would topple soon enough, due to a lack of strong roots. Yang energy that has forgotten where its strength comes from becomes brittle and unstable. In its instability, it will lose confidence and either collapse or puff itself up into the kind of arrogant and aggressive posturing that has led us into numerous wars and conflicts.

Over-identification with Yin

Though western culture as a whole over-identifies with the yang emphasis on continuous growth, many people, especially those who think of themselves as 'alternative', have, for that precise reason, become imbalanced on the opposite flank. Eschewing yang virtues of striving and desire for success, they have become stuck in passivity, powerlessness and lack of direction or ambition. 'I am perfect as I am' can become an unconscious way of colluding with the part of ourselves that resists or is frightened of growth or change. Imagine the acorn saying, 'No, I won't open, I'm perfect as I am.' Eventually it would rot. You *are* perfect as you are *and* you need to grow. Here again we have the balancing act: acceptance without complacency, growth without rushing. As we often say, 'Don't push and don't hold back.'

Many years ago, one of our then students, a cellist called Matthew Barley, helped us reframe the words 'work' and 'effort'. In our attempts to help ourselves and others relax and let go of the punitive effects of an old-style yang 'Succeed or else!' attitude, we had thrown the baby out with the bathwater. In our dance workshops we often used to say, 'Let it happen, no effort,' as if effort was a problem. Matthew reminded us of the value of work and effort through his own experience of the sustained work and effort necessary in becoming a cellist, and we got the message!

In the same vein, Sarah Harlow, a yoga teacher, talks about balancing what she calls 'honest effort' within an overall respect and graceful surrender to the actual limits of our physical capacity.

Susannah: *Years ago I had a vision of myself making music and singing. I had no idea how this would happen. I had always had music in me and would lie in bed with fantastical symphonic angelic music sweeping me into heaven. But though I learned to play the piano, I resisted learning theory and so had no language in which to communicate my inner musical world to anyone else. I had the idea that if it was meant to happen, it would, and the vague fantasy that Peter Gabriel would hear me singing in a pub and ask me to sing on one of his albums, but that was as far as it went.*

Then I read the cover notes on one of Lorena McKennit's albums which spoke of her level of commitment and 'sweat' for her art before she ever received any recognition. I finally realized I could probably wait forever for Peter Gabriel (especially as I don't generally go to pubs!) and that if I wanted to make music then I needed to assume the authority and responsibility myself.

Once I did, and began learning music theory and studying singing and voice production, I met some extraordinary collaborators who helped me begin to manifest the music that wanted to come through me. Four albums later, I am still learning, still practising, still balancing honest effort with surrender, and am so happy that I stepped forward.

Over the years we have realized again and again that we could wait forever for someone to give us permission to be or do something. But knowing when you are ready to pick up your crown and take responsibility for being your own authority is a matter of timing and experience. The trick is balance. We need the acceptance of where we are and the intention of where we want to go.

Here's a recipe to help you to get to know your inner yang and inner yin energy better and to bring them into balance.

Inner Yin and Yang

- **Intention:** To experience the inner yin and yang and the dance between them.

- **Purpose:** To get to know these cornerstones of the Movement Medicine journey.

This meditation is good to do after dancing, or after a walk, or yoga, when you feel grounded and connected to your body.

Part I: Inner Yin
Sit comfortably. Close your eyes and bring your attention into the flesh and muscles of your body, allowing yourself to relax, feeling your physicality and your breath.

Move gently, from the inside out, feeling the inner textures, imagining the breath permeating every part of your body and letting everything soften and gently open and widen.

Take yourself on a little journey through your body. As you do so, pay attention to your inner landscape. Whatever you find, let it be. Say 'yes' to it, kindly accepting things as they are. Imagine yourself as a wise, gentle, warm mother taking everything into her arms and holding it in love. Notice your body posture and allow yourself to become conscious of the support of the ground beneath you.

Now, in whatever way feels good to you, ask the universal divine mother to hold *you*. She has many names in different traditions. Maybe you have a name for her. She resonates mercy, compassion, love, acceptance and many other things. Maybe she feels very remote, maybe very vivid and close. You can cultivate her presence within and around you by becoming still and practising this loving embrace of yourself and your condition, just as you are.

Find the physical shape that helps you feel this self-love and acceptance and be in it for a few moments, breathing it in. We will call this shape your 'mudra of acceptance'.

From this ground of acceptance, what other qualities, shapes and expressions of yin energy can you imagine, invoke and embody?

Part II: Inner Yang

Now shift your attention to your skeleton. Feel the strength and uprightness of your spine. Allow your chest and ribs to widen, your crown to rise, your tailbone to drop and your heart to rise towards the sun. Feel your inner warrior, your strength, determination and focus. Concentrate on the warmth of your breath and open your eyes, finding a point on which to focus. Here is your sense of direction, movement and determination.

Breathe into this aspect of yourself, saying 'yes' to your sense of direction and intention. Ask the universal divine father to strengthen you, to support you and to empower your sense of intention. He resonates strength, truth, justice, love and many other qualities. He has many names in different traditions. Maybe you have a name for him. Maybe he feels very remote, maybe very vivid and close. You can cultivate his presence within and around you by becoming still and practising this attitude and posture of upright, open-hearted strength and focus.

Notice your posture, and then, standing or sitting, amplify it, strengthening the sense of the heartful warrior within who gives you the courage to become all that you can become. We will call this shape your 'mudra of intention'.

Hold this position for a few moments, letting some deep breaths bring vitality to your sense of intention and saying a big '*Yes!*' to your direction.

What other qualities, shapes and expressions of yang energy can you imagine, invoke and embody?

Part III: The Meeting of Inner Yin and Yang

Now slowly shift between these mudras of acceptance and intention. Feel the interplay between these shapes and energies. Let them support and strengthen each other. Take your time with this and enjoy the life energy that always arises in the dynamic interplay of polarity.

Finally, come to rest in a shape between the two, allowing the energies to mingle and meet within you.

Bring your meditation to a close by bowing to the divine yin and yang and thanking the unique mixture of the two that you are.

We recommend taking a little quiet time to make notes and drink a glass of water before continuing with your day.

So, now you are more in touch with the forces of creation that you were born with, let's move on to the next steps on this 9 Gateways journey and the creation of your remarkable life.

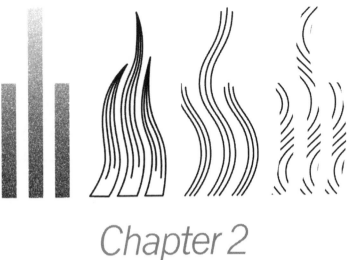

Chapter 2
The Four Elements

'Nothing is more revealing than movement.'
Martha Graham

Life on our planet is born of the meeting between the earth, the sun, the water and the air. It began in the primal soup of the waters as the energy of the sun met the minerals of the earth and the molecules of the water. The air (atmosphere) appeared as a result of the development of the first life forms. Today the dance of the four elements of earth, air, fire and water is a vital part of photosynthesis, our metabolism and the mutual exchange of carbon dioxide and oxygen between plants and mammals which sustains life on Earth.

The Elements in Movement Medicine Practice

For healing to become manifest we need to allow consciousness and compassion to move through the physical, emotional and mental levels, so that they can inform our experience and our actions. In order to do this we need to remember that the physical body is the temple and the playground of the spirit. And for this, we need allies. In Movement Medicine practice we dance with the elements as our allies.

The wonderful thing about working with the four elements is that they provide teachings to which each of us has direct access. They exist in a very real way both inside us and outside us as part of the fabric of our day-to-day existence. So working with the elements both in movement and through ritual brings us deeply into relationship with our own nature as well as with nature itself.

As well as physical presences, the four elements are an excellent metaphorical language for describing some of the different qualities of being human. For instance, if you think of your friends, you can probably instinctively feel whether someone is more watery or fiery, more earthy or airy. Through working with the elements we can each balance our inner elemental wheel. This has practical benefits in all areas of life.

Susannah: *The waitress in our local cinema café told me that she couldn't bear to see most films because they made her cry too much. She didn't mind crying, but found it too much to dissolve into floods of tears each time she watched a film. Obviously she has a big heart, but, as she said herself, her watery-ness often gets in the way of being*

*strong enough to do what she wants to do. She would
benefit from a little more fire and earth and a bit less water.
Then, as well as being more balanced in life in general, she
could enjoy a few more films!*

Each element offers us different qualities and through exploring
them in movement we increase the possibilities we have at our
disposal. The more we pay attention to them in our practice,
the more we will become aware of them when we eat, light the
oven, take a shower or take a deep breath. Our ability to learn
from them and to dance as them provides us with the strong
foundations we need for the dancer within to become grounded
and to gain free access to a full spectrum of possibility.

A Map of Consciousness

There are many different traditions that work with the four
elements in a mandala, and Movement Medicine does so too.
The Movement Medicine mandala is a map of consciousness.
Our intention is to continue to learn to embody and live that
consciousness and to guide our students to do the same, each
in their own unique way.

Each tradition attributes the elements to the four directions
in its own way. For us, earth sits in the south, fire in the east,
water in the west and air in the north.

Each time we come to dance, we visualize ourselves at the
centre of our own mandala and call on the help of each
element and the spirit or guardian of that element. By the end
of the first part of this book, having partaken of the recipes
on offer, you will be able to do the same.

The Dancer Within

Every time we dance, we begin with the meditation of giving ourselves back to the dancer within us. What we mean by the word 'dancer' is the part of us, the energy body, that is already free, fluid and in motion. It already knows how to move from the deepest intelligence within us.

People sometimes ask us, 'Don't you get bored of doing the same meditation again and again?' The answer is no, we don't. Every day we are different and every day the dancer within may open another vista in the endlessly fascinating landscape of the soul. Apart from that, this meditation grounds us and gives us the opportunity to check in, much like checking the air pressure in the tyres of your bicycle or car before you take a journey.

With any movement-based exercise, it is always important to listen out for anything uncomfortable and to move within any limitations your body has. These need not hamper you. We have seen some of the most remarkable dances coming from people who were physically injured or had some movement disability. Thomas Krysiza, from Denmark, has danced for years with muscular dystrophy. He wears a helmet and we used to joke that he had single-handedly transformed our work into an extreme sport. Another student, Erika Seitz from Germany, who was in her sixties at the time, once came to a workshop while recovering from a broken leg. We will never forget the grace and eloquence of a dance that came through her whilst she was sitting on a chair at the side of the room. Each of us can find the dance that comes from within us, whatever our circumstances. So are you ready to meet the dancer in you?

Awakening the Dancer Within

- **Intention:** To meet and begin to trust the dancer inside you.

- **Purpose:** To know that beyond your inhibitions, patterns and stories, there is a part of you that is already free, full of vitality and connected to a deep source of intelligence and peace.

You will need 20 minutes of uninterrupted time for this recipe. You can use gentle music or do it in silence. It is on our CD *Movement Medicine Meditations 1: For the Dance of Life*.

Attention, breath and allowing the body to melt into movement are what is important. The size of the movement is not. Very small, conscious, interior movement is valuable for developing awareness, life and presence. If you find your body naturally wanting to make bigger movements or gestures, let it, but you do not need to do so. There is the possibility of great pleasure in the physical sensation of your own body moving. So let yourself feel it!

Standing, bring your attention inside your body. Allow your body to breathe naturally and freely. As you breathe, visualize your roots, ground yourself and make a connection to the living energy of the Earth beneath you.

Imagine you are being lifted gently from the top of your head towards the sky. Let the back of your neck lengthen and reach your arms up for a few moments if you want to. This allows the backbone to lengthen.

Bringing the arms down, let the backbone rest in your hips and let the weight of your body drop down through the soles of your feet.

Slowly begin to move your attention through your body and as you come to each part, invite breath and gentle movement to awaken the possibility of pleasure in the physical sensation of your own body.

Start with the spine. Move gently from within to feel the whole length of your spine, all the way from your neck down to your tailbone. Imagine you have a tail. Feels its weight. It may be like a dog's tail or the tail of a Tyrannosaurus Rex, a horse, a lion, a mouse or another animal. Try to get a visual sense of it. Try to feel it. Say to yourself: 'I give my spine back to the dancer within me.'

Moving very gently, from the inside out, allow yourself to feel the texture of the muscles on either side of your spine, sending your mind into the spaces between the vertebrae. Let your 'tail' help you feel your spine all the way down. This may feel strange. You may feel numb, or pain, or pleasure. Your ability to feel your interior space is a skill. It will grow with practice. Your brain and body will respond to your attention. So be patient and gentle with yourself. Keep returning your mind to your inner landscape and inviting pleasure, breath and movement.

From your spine, find your hips, feeling how your spine is linked to your hips via the sacrum. Filling the bowl of your hips with your attention, let them melt into motion. Allow the movement to help you feel your hips from the inside and say to yourself: 'I give my hips back to the dancer within me.' Let your hips be free to show you how they move, while staying conscious of your backbone. As you shift your attention to the different parts of your body, you are step by step filling your whole body with your awareness and the freedom to move.

From your hips, let your attention fill your whole torso, moving gently from the inside to help yourself feel your sides, your front and your back, your ribs and the muscles between them. Keep tuning to the 'pleasure' station.

Then find your shoulder blades. Let them slide over your ribs, feeling the space between your shoulders. And then feel the connection between your shoulder blades and your shoulders. Acknowledge their condition. Maybe they feel stiff or heavy, or free and winged. Within their condition, whatever it is, allow them to melt into gentle movement and then extend your attention slowly down your forearms, elbows, lower arms, wrists and hands and fingertips. Say out loud: 'I give my arms and shoulders and hands back to the dancer within me,' and let them move!

Then bring your attention up into your neck, again respecting its condition, and let movement and breath move through the inner textures, whatever they are. From your neck, feel into the physical sensations of your face, eyes, nose, mouth, throat and scalp. Once your skull and face are moving, bring in your fingers to move in a duet with them. 'I give my head and neck back to the dancer within me.'

Now let yourself feel the full landscape of your upper body and hips and from there feel into your legs. Find out how you can move to literally sense your anatomy.

Feel how your upper leg bone connects with your hips. Feel into the muscles in your legs, all the way down to your knees, lower legs, ankles and feet. Take time to feel into the inner structural subtlety of your ankles, feet and toes and how they meet the floor. Let your feet move and play. 'I give my legs, knees, ankles and feet back to the dancer within me.'

Now, including your hands, your feet, your tail, your head and everything in between, engage your torso and let your whole body move from the inside out.

Your whole body will be in motion now and you can move between quietly listening to the interior of your body and more expressive movement. Take some time to enjoy yourself. Give yourself back to the dancer you are. Before you know it, you'll be breathing deeply and moving freely.

Coming to rest in your own time, take a moment to sense your body as a whole. This is your own ground, your anchor. The dancer in you is awake and ready to help you in the manifestation of your dreams.

Congratulations! You have embarked upon the Movement Medicine journey.

Chapter 3
Earth

'We did not come into this world. We came out of it like buds out of branches and butterflies out of cocoons. We are a natural product of this Earth and, if we turn out to be intelligent beings, then it can only be because we are the fruits of an intelligent Earth.'

Lyall Watson, *Gifts of Unknown Things*

We think of the spirit of the Earth as a living being who treats us with enormous generosity and patience. We refer to this spirit as 'she', but please don't feel limited by this. It's up to you to find out for yourself, through your own direct connection, how you experience the different elements. There are many practices designed to help you to make this connection. For us, the way is a combination of dance and ritual.

In the West, we tend to ignore the wisdom of the Earth and treat the planet as a resource to be used. In parallel with this there has been a great deal of pressure to ignore the wisdom of our physical bodies. This happened first through the Church's determination to separate body and spirit. It has continued more recently through the mass marketing of the image of the perfect body that so many of us feel under such enormous pressure to live up to. All of this takes us away from our inherent ability to listen to the intelligence inside us. We are encouraged to live life in our heads – in effect, as far away from our feet as possible. The consequences of this are dire for us as individuals and as a human race. There is very little in this world that grows without roots. And many of us have lost our roots. This in turn means being cut off from a major source of strength and interconnectedness, namely the energy and nourishment of the Great Mother beneath us.

We wonder how different our experience of life would be if we were to begin each day by thanking the living Earth beneath our feet for creating the conditions so that we can live. We don't mean this in a religious sense, but more in the way that we might thank an elder or a good friend for the goodness they bring into our lives. Like any relationship, our relationship with the Earth deepens through the attention we give to it.

One of the deepest experiences we had during our apprenticeship in Peru was receiving a vision of the spirit of the Earth. We saw her as an enormous force, undulating, tender, wild and infinitely loving and patient.

In the books written by Victor Megre about the Siberian recluse and wise woman Anastasia, the main character on whom the books are based tells us that just as we feel the presence of a mosquito on our skin, so the Earth feels everything we do. She says that when a human being places their hands on the Earth with love and gratitude, the Earth feels it deeply and is supported by it. Recently, we have spent time paying attention to the more sensitive side of the ground beneath our feet and have been very moved by the love and connection we have felt.

> **Ya'Acov:** *As I knelt down on a recent Saturday morning to put my hands on the cold morning earth and simply give a little love and gratitude, I felt so small and insignificant. And then I remembered the quote on our kitchen wall that exhorts us to 'Risk our insignificance' and act boldly with love. And so I did. As my heart warmed, so did my hands, and I saw a glow of connection like a silver latticed web which seemed to appear out of nowhere and went right through my own body and everything else. The sun was slanting through the trees, everything around me brightened, and for a while, I disappeared in the autumn light.*

Earth Dancing

It's time to take the relationship with the dancer in you a step further. We're going to guide you through the creative task of connecting with the earth of your own body and the Earth under your feet. Through the dance and simple ritual, we're going to help you to come into an awareness of the Earth as a great being of which you are part. Finding your own way of dancing with the earth element and, through this, coming back to the body as the home for your spirit can bring a deep sense of safety, support and spaciousness.

Lyall Watson, whom we quote at the beginning of this chapter, says that just as the mother's heartbeat comforts and supports a baby both in and out of the womb, so there is a relationship between the pulse of the Earth's magnetic field and the predominant rhythm of the human brain. They both fluctuate between 8 and 16 times a second. This means that we all have this sustaining resonance with the living Earth, or the Great Mother, whatever the quality of the relationship with our human mother may be or may have been.

Here are a couple of recipes to help you to come into a deeper relationship with the earth element and, through this, find more roots and ground for the journey ahead.

Earth Cradle

- **Intention:** To tune into and receive support from the Earth Mother.

- **Purpose:** To find the safety to relax deeply in order to flower again.

This is done outdoors and is best done when the weather is warm and the earth not too wet! Find somewhere where you can lie down or curl up in an earth hollow. Sometimes you will find these naturally occurring in the woods, on the moors or in a wild meadow. Or, if you have a garden, you can scoop one out of the earth for yourself. Line it with a wool or cotton blanket, or wear clothes that you won't mind getting a bit earthy or grassy if necessary.

Kneeling by the hollow, speak respectfully to the Earth Mother, asking her to hold you, to cradle you, to nurture you. Then go on in. Get comfortable. Put yourself in her arms. Let her hold you. Let your weight go. Sink into the ground like a kitten nestling into its mother.

Breathing deeply and slowly, feel yourself tuning into the Earth's heartbeat, the Earth's stillness. Ask the Earth Mother to help you reconnect with this great being of which you are part. Ask for healing, ask for forgiveness, or simply ask to rest in her arms.

Maybe you will meditate, maybe you will slumber. Receive the blessing of the Earth Mother's presence.

When it is time for you to leave, say thank you and leave a (biodegradable!) offering as a blessing for the place.

Susannah: *Many times I have gone to an earth cradle when I have been sad or depleted. I have always emerged feeling reassured, renewed, as if I really have been in my mother's lap. Trusting the Earth to hold me has been part of coming to trust femininity, softness, slowness and gentleness. It's so good to feel the richness of life in my body, in every toe, in every vertebra, in the breath, in the sweet smell of the earth and the sound of the wind stirring the leaves.*

There is a beautiful relationship between the earth of your body and the body of the Earth. It is a love affair that is called gravity. This recipe invites you to 'go with' gravity to help you feel this connection and then to take this connectedness into your dance.

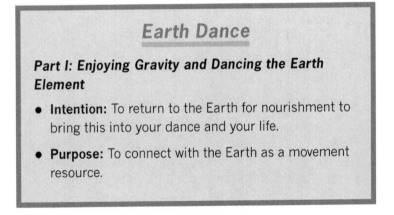

Earth Dance

Part I: Enjoying Gravity and Dancing the Earth Element

- **Intention:** To return to the Earth for nourishment to bring this into your dance and your life.

- **Purpose:** To connect with the Earth as a movement resource.

This is usually done indoors, though you can do it outside somewhere where you won't be disturbed. Find somewhere quiet with enough space to roll about on the floor without hitting anything. You can either put on some appropriate music or do this in silence.

Find a way that feels right to you to pay your respects to the Earth, ask her for her support and guidance in the future and thank her for her support and guidance in the past. You may feel silly doing this. It doesn't matter. Opening to the possibility that there is an Earth intelligence holding all of us and actively communicating with her will open the way for new connections to be made.

Now lie down slowly in whatever posture feels good. Take some breaths to feel your whole body releasing the tension used in holding itself up. You can let go now. To do this, it may help to take a paradoxical remedy, so try tensing yourself up as tightly as you can. Tense all your muscles – face, bum, shoulders, hands, legs, feet – and hold it, and then let go and breathe out.

Lying there now, breathe as slowly and as deeply as your body wants to. Give it permission to drink in the breath as if it were thirsty for it. Find yourself a benevolent mantra such as 'I am safe here, I can be here, be me, simply as I am' or 'I am a beloved son/daughter of the Earth. Now I can let go.'

As you say your mantra, let your consciousness gently wander through the interior of your body, inviting the breath to open and soften each part.

When you are ready, begin to move, slowly, luxuriously,

lazily rolling and stretching. See if you can let the whole surface of your body touch the floor. Let each part soften and melt into the floor as it touches it and imagine yourself drinking in the living energy, or *prana*, of the Earth through this contact. All the while, keep breathing, imagining the breath infusing the whole body.

Do this for at least 10 minutes, pausing and resting when you need to. This recipe is about awareness, not acrobatics. If you are skinny and your bones feel tender when they come into contact with the floor, don't bruise yourself. Go extra slowly and softly and use a couple of yoga mats if you need to. Pain is not the name of the game!

When you are ready, come to stillness again and rest for a few minutes lying curled up on your side. Then slowly sit up. Touch the Earth with your hands.

Slowly come up to standing and once there, imagine your feet opening to connect with the ground. See how fluid and heavy you can allow your body to feel as you stand upright.

Now allow your body to begin to melt gently into motion, from the inside out. Starting with the bowl of your pelvis, let your body, your living piece of land, move. You are not concerned with looking good. Your attention is on feeling the textures and sensations of earth and following the impulses of the body as the dancer inside you explores this element.

Body part by body part, travel through your whole body, inviting the dancer within you to bring everything into circulation. Your dance may be tiny and interior or large and more expressive. Explore how the earth element moves through you today. You are looking for a sense of grounding and the dances that will allow you to experience a living connection with this element inside and outside you. Feeling, following, sensing the ground beneath you and the earth within you, you are the Earth dancing.

Finally come to rest, thanking the earth of your body and the body of the Earth.

Guardians

In order to deepen the experience of standing and dancing at the centre of your circle, we are going to find a guardian for each direction of your mandala. In the shamanic paradigm, these guardians are called spirits. In a more western therapeutic paradigm, we might call them archetypes. It doesn't matter. What does matter is that we extend and deepen our experience by inviting the more image-orientated right side of the brain to help us gain a stronger sense of these elemental forces. Over time, this brings us more confidence and a stronger sense of dancing at the centre of our own circle.

Ya'Acov: *Walking in the forest this morning, I was saying thank you to all the guardians that I've been working with over the years. As I was doing so, I felt a tangible presence in the air all around me and I immediately felt uplifted and fortified. I remembered that it had taken me many years to get a sense of the reality of these energies and that when I began, they were little more than amorphous ideas. Over* *the years, as I have danced more deeply, my relationships with these beings has grown ever more intimate and strong. I am truly grateful that I was able to suspend my disbelief for just long enough those many years ago. That tiny window gave me the space to allow my imagination to build a bridge between my rational mind and the little flame of possibility inside me that remembered that there was more to life than met the eye.*

Earth Dance (continued)

Part II: Meeting the Spirit of the Earth

- **Intention:** To connect with the guardian for the south of your personal medicine wheel.

- **Purpose:** To build a strong sense of your own circle and connect to the resources that will support you as you continue your journey.

Now that you have been moving, have a sense of your relationship to the earth element and have taken steps to further embody this, it is time to meet the spirit of the earth. She has many beautiful manifestations. Some call her Shekinah, others Pacha Mama, others Gaia. What is important is your relationship with her.

Still moving, we invite you to look to the south and ask this spirit to come and dance with you in the south of your circle. True *seeing* can be felt through the body, seen through the eyes or heard as words or music. Trust the senses within you that extend beyond your rational thought process and focus your mind, your movement, your entire being on asking the spirit of the earth to show up in your circle today.

When we are humble enough to ask, spirit always answers, though not always in ways that we recognize or understand. So be patient and feel your love for the living energy of the Great Mother. Put your hands on the ground, speak to her, dance with her. Feel free to ask her any questions you may have, such as: 'How should I best look after this body, this temple for the spirit?' or 'How can I deepen my connection with you?'

We have a friend who had no faith in the spiritual nature of life. His wife felt concern for the Earth and her wellbeing. She wanted to do her bit and get her household to recycle what they could, but he insisted that it wasn't worth it. By chance, he found himself in the Amazon rainforest on a project and was invited to participate in a ceremony. Not wishing to be impolite, he accepted. During the ceremony, he was astonished to meet the spirit of the earth in the form of the Queen of the Forest. Expecting some great mystical revelation, he asked her: 'What should I do?' Her answer was simple: 'Recycle!' He returned, humbled, and did as he was told.

What advice does the spirit of the earth have for you today?

Once you are done with your dance, thank her, release her and ask her to show up again when next you call her or in your dreams. It may be helpful to find an image or object, or make one, that reminds you of her presence.

So, we have begun the creative task of constructing your own dancing medicine wheel. Now that we have the container, let's build a fire in it and continue our journey.

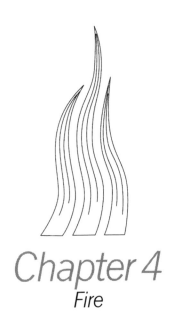

Chapter 4
Fire

'Become like the sun. Nourish this ideal until it becomes such a part of you that your entire being is set aflame and illuminated by it. This will make all the seeds of the divine life grow in you, and, without dwelling on it or even thinking about it, you will manifest what is best in you. The only truth worth seeking is the spiritual sun. The moment it shines in you, you become like the earth in springtime, when all of nature returns to life.'

Omraam Mikhaël Aïvanhov

During our travels and studies, we have had the good fortune to meet many fine teachers and shamans. They have all had some things in common, such as a reverence for the natural world, the spirit world and the world of the ancestors. They have seen the elements as sacred and considered a healthy relationship to them vital for wellbeing. We have been inspired by many ceremonies in which prayers were offered to the Divine

Feminine and her manifestation as the Earth, and to the Divine Masculine and his manifestation as the sun. We often ask: 'Do you have a message for our people?' And we have often had the same response: 'Tell them to keep the sacred fire burning.'

In this chapter, we refer to the spirit of the fire as 'he', but feel free to use this or discard it as you feel appropriate. Please don't get sidetracked by concerns about the gender of the elements. Earth is earth and fire is fire, and it's up to you to find your own language and create a relationship with the fire that is true for you.

The Power of the Sun

The sun is the source of life energy on Earth. The spirit of the fire is also vital for our wellbeing and we experience it as an extraordinary gift. It illuminates everything, provides warmth and light, comfort and protection, and helps us to burn through what we no longer need.

Fire is a powerful energy of transformation. Each of us has 'firepower' and we either learn to use it responsibly or it becomes a source of destruction in our lives. Too much and we are destroyed by our own activity. Too little and we die. In our movement practice, we make a link between the sun, the fire and the energy of intention and evolution, and we dance to embody a creative relationship with this force.

Fire is part of us at a fundamental level. In each cell of our bodies are mitochondria which 'burn' glucose and release its energy for all our life processes, whether they are running a marathon, thinking about the nature of life, keeping our heart beating or repairing our skin. In the mitochondrial combustion engine, glucose and oxygen are transformed into water and carbon dioxide and a release of energy which is stored for use by the body in a biochemical called adenosine tri-phosphate, or ATP for short. Where does this energy come from? Trace it back: glucose comes from food, all of which, whether vegetable or animal eventually, via the food chain, comes from plants, which grow via photosynthesis. So it comes from the sun. Quite literally, your life energy is the sun burning and shining through your zillion cells, whether you are throwing a javelin, feeding your baby, thinking, singing or reading this book.

The higher your metabolic rate, the warmer you are and the more solar energy you are converting. We recognize this when we say someone is 'fiery'. They are! That high-energy combustible being is plugging into and converting a lot of solar energy into movement, sound and heat.

Firepower

Solar input and output (or metabolic rate) connect with the strength and solar energy of the quintessential warrior that is inside each of us. This firepower is intoxicating, powerful and potentially addictive. Don't we love it! We love to rev that engine and feel the power kick in as we shift into gear. We love to ride a strong horse fast across the moors. We love the big fireworks, the bonfires, the exultation of speed and power. Fire is sexy, seductive, and once it's started, it can be hard to control. What we do with it is a question of awareness.

Susannah: *During one of our first ceremonies with shamans in the rainforest of Peru, I felt called to stand up. Feeling the lion in my chest and the warrior in my arms,*

I felt powerful, dignified, eager, balanced and energized, ready for anything. Then immediately I was instructed, 'Now bow and dedicate this energy.' I spent the next hours bobbing up and down between a lion's warrior stance and deep bowing, dedicating this energy to life. It was serious, wonderful and rather amusing. My mysterious teacher was very clear. As soon as one energy had been established, I was instructed to shift to the other: 'Now stand up! Now, bow down and dedicate!'

And it made so much sense. Firepower is such a strength, but held without consciousness, without connection and the intent to serve a creative purpose, it can be dangerous. I felt the wisdom of my own psyche holding my energy in check until I was ready to dedicate it with precision. You don't give a young child a big hammer until they know what it is for and how to use it.

Fire energy makes us grow. It is reflected in the growth part of the natural cycle; in spring and summer, the plants grow towards the sun. The trouble is, we are out of balance. We want to grow and grow and grow. We want more and more and more. Our human population grows and grows. We all want to consume more. The insatiable ever-growing appetite of humans is consuming the world. Where is it leading us, our addiction to the firepower of continuous growth and energy consumption? It's no surprise that the world is getting hotter.

Susannah: *Another time in a ceremony I saw tiny mischievous creatures which I called 'fire elves'. They breathed out fire, and each fiery breath became a whirling blade with which they were sawing down trees at the edge of a rainforest. They were gleeful. Not mean, not evil, not angry, just revelling in the power of their fire. As I watched* *them, their joy in their unbridled expression was infectious and I couldn't help but celebrate with them.*

Shockingly slowly, I realized that they were cutting down the trees and what that meant for all of us. I began to weep. I saw how easy it could be to be innocently and ignorantly intoxicated by firepower and to be unconscious of the effect of this energy on the environment around us.

Maybe, like the fire elves, our ignorance is of an innocent nature. In the nineteenth century we discovered enormous power in the Industrial Revolution and we have been gleefully stretching and flexing our muscles ever since. It is high time we woke up and balanced this power with awareness and responsibility.

A Fine Balance

A common trap here is to assume that fire energy is the problem. Then we throw the baby out with the bathwater. The key is to match power with consciousness, strength with sensibility, warriorhood with service. Many indigenous cultures are exquisitely aware of this balance in their education of their young people in this regard, especially their young men, harnessing their firepower for the common good. Fire energy without wise guidance finds its own purpose. It has to express itself somehow.

Ya'Acov: *In my early twenties, I was an active anti-nuclear campaigner. As the dawn came close on a misty late summer night, I and nine other men were cutting down* fencing around a Scottish military base that was connected to the Faslane nuclear submarine programme. We were part of an international gathering to oppose the building of nuclear submarines on the loch at Faslane. Through non-violent direct action we intended to highlight the levels of radioactivity in the loch. Being a men's group of ardent feminists, we had named ourselves 'the Wee Willy Wimpos and the Wailing Wizards of Gondwanaland'. I'd like to tell you that the name was a joke, but it will tell you more about how I and many men in those times were thinking to tell you that in fact we were deadly serious. We saw our firepower as dangerous and destructive, and we rejected it. In so doing, we projected it all out onto the big bad world of the military. We were the good guys and they were the bad guys who needed reforming and educating.

As you can imagine, the blend of my sweet non-violence and state-of-the-art shiny red bolt-cutters didn't go down too well when we were arrested. The more I smiled in my practised non-violent way, the more violent my arresting officer became. He dragged me off the roof that we had unfurled our banner on, all the while nudging me closer to the edge and telling me that it would be a real shame if I 'just happened to slip and fall off'.

Four days in a cell in Maryhill police station gave me plenty of time to think about the violent conduct of our arresting officer. I got a glimmer of the realization that whatever I didn't own inside myself, I was destined to meet and do battle with outside myself. I was beginning to see that a sweet passive-aggressive smile was no replacement for the red-blooded fire in me that wanted to shout out loud for freedom and justice. That was the beginning of the process that led me to the dance and eventually to the relief of finding a place where that energy could move safely and find its creative expression and integration. I cannot imagine now how I ever survived without it.

Playing with Fire

A few years ago, we did some work with a very fiery teacher from Mexico called Victor Sanchez. He had been asked to carry the teachings of the Wirrarika people into the world. He was a bear of a man, warm-hearted and passionate about his mission and our possibilities as human beings.

One night, we were all invited to a fire ceremony. Victor lit the fire in a very purposeful way, laying a 'pillow' for what he called Tatewari, or Grandfather Fire, to rest his head. He then placed a number of logs across the pillow, all facing east, and asked each of us to take a 'prayer stick', introduce ourselves to the fire and then lay our offerings in the same direction. This was important, as it was a symbol of collective intent working in the same direction.

One at a time, we stepped forward and whispered our prayers in a very polite western European manner. There was a hush around the fire and then Victor and his assistant stepped forward to make their offerings. In unison, at the top of their voices, they shouted out: 'Do you know, Grandfather, how much we love you? Do you know how grateful we are for your warmth here tonight?'

Once we'd all got over the culture shock, we all felt the genuine beauty of their relationship with the living spirit of the fire. Victor told us that since his teacher, an old shaman, had introduced him to the fire, he had never been lonely. He always carried a small candle with him so that he could sit down and have a good chat with his grandfather whenever he needed to and wherever he was on his travels. He told us that there were numerous opportunities during the day to deepen our relationship with the spirit of the fire and we realized that it was true. Starting the car, cooking our food and hearing the central heating firing up are all moments when we can realize just how important fire is to us on a daily basis.

Victor gave us another ceremony to perform to strengthen our connection to our inner fire and the power of conscious intent. We'll share it with you here as part of a fire ceremony recipe. There is something about sitting by the fire that awakens an ancient sense of peace and connection. Try this.

Rising Sun Fire Ceremony

- **Intention:** To give thanks to the fire and ask it to be your teacher, guide and inspiration on your spiritual journey.

- **Purpose:** To feel the passion in your heart and find the courage to clearly state your intent.

This is best done outdoors if possible. First of all, whenever you are meditating or performing a ceremony somewhere in nature, it is important to ask the spirit of the place for permission to be there. Different people feel the answers to this sort of question in different ways. Sometimes you get a feeling such as warmth in the heart if the answer is 'yes', or a feeling of unease or even dread if the answer is 'no'. It's important to remember that you are a guest in that place. We usually take a portable altar with us containing a few sacred objects that have special meaning for us. We suggest you do the same. Simplicity is good.

Find a private place in nature where it is safe (and not illegal) to light a fire, preferably with a view to the east. If you don't have any experience of how to light and tend a fire safely, make sure you get some advice before you go. You need to be able to make noise, so bear that in mind when choosing your place. It's worth taking a trip to somewhere where you'll be able to do this, but if this is impossible, preparing a fire in a fireplace at home or in your garden or a friend's would be fine.

Go to your chosen spot a few hours before dawn and prepare your fire with care and attention, making a suitable place for your grandfather to visit. As you light your fire, introduce yourself, thank the fire and state your intention. Sometimes, the hardest thing is to ask for help and guidance, but with a little fire energy, you'll be able to. Ask the fire to teach you about the fire within you.

Once your fire is lit, your task is simple and enjoyable: watch it dancing. Notice the different phases it moves through: slow and deep, fast and dynamic, magical and unpredictable, still and peaceful. Learn what you can about the many different ways your fire expresses itself. Ask yourself and ask the fire, 'If the fire within me were in optimum health, how would that be expressed in my life? How could I better use the fire energy within me? How could I better honour the fire as a creative force in my life?'

Do all of this before the sun rises. Ideally, the fire will have arrived at its sparkly ember stage just as the sun starts to appear.

Now we'll move on to the ceremony we received from Victor. Every day, as the sun rises, we have an opportunity to begin our life again. A new sunrise is like a new canvas, and beginning the day with gratitude is a powerful statement of intent. Energy follows attention, so taking the time to focus your energy in this way is good practice.

As you see the sun beginning to arise in the east, start to run on the spot with your arms by your side, lifting your knees as high as they can go without hurting yourself. Start slowly and pace yourself so that once the full globe of the sun has risen from the horizon, you are running at maximum speed on the spot. At this point, stop running, spread your arms wide and open your chest and your heart and shout out your gratitude to the sun and your commitment to allowing the fire within you to express its nature in its full range and power *and* with full responsibility and sensitivity. Send these statements like arrows from your heart into the heart of the sun. Try saying this incantation out loud and from your heart, or find your own words for it: 'I am a child of the sun and it is my nature to shine!'

Make sure your fire is safe to leave, or put it out if there is any danger, and thank the fire and the place. You'll probably be quite fired up for your day!

Now you've had a chance to learn from the fire outside you, let's give the dancer within you the opportunity to discover how the fire within you dances.

Fire Dance

Part I: Dancing your Fire

- **Intention:** To tune into your firepower and direct it.
- **Purpose:** To balance firepower with consciousness.

Find some appropriate music or feel free to do this in silence. Create a space in which to work and get yourself present in body, heart and mind through your Movement Medicine practice or any other tool you have.

Stand facing the sun. It's great if it is shining on you. Close your eyes and feel its warmth and light. In your mind's eye see the rays of light running straight between you and the sun. Allow yourself to feel the sun shining his light on you and on life, making the Earth fertile. Offer the sun a gesture of respect and thanks for giving you life.

Let the sun's heat and light ignite your own fire. Feel it alight and burning in every cell. If you can't feel it, imagine it!

Breathe on your inner fire and begin to move, feeling the fire in your loins, the strength in your muscles, the sun burning through you. Invite the warrior in you to rise.

Take the time to explore how this energy expresses itself through you. Remember how fire burns. Sometimes it is deep and still. Sometimes it burns bright and strong and fast. Let the fire in you rise. Use your voice. Allow your passion. Feel the deep quiet strength of the fire and the more direct, expressive energy of the fire. 'I am as I am,' 'I am free,' 'I want more!' 'I want to live' and 'I am strong!' are great mantras for this energy. Imagine you have a sword and let yourself dance with it, cutting through the illusions of the past with consciousness and compassion. Imagine your whole circle is burning bright with healing flames.

Feel your power and then come to a still pose in the shape of your own fire energy. 'I am here! I am a child of the sun and it is my nature to *shine!*' Stand tall. Permit pride, a sense of nobility and dignity. Now bow and make a gesture to dedicate this energy to your own highest purpose, however you feel it now. If you aren't specific about this yet, don't worry. Intending to discover how to use this firepower as an ally in your life is a good place to start.

Go back and forth between these shapes, concentrating on the physical sensation of the body moving, the feeling in your heart and whatever words fit as a mantra.

When you come to rest, take a moment to stand and feel the inner tree, feeling the link with the earth from your feet and, raising your arms for a moment, feeling your branches rise towards the sun. And then, letting your arms rest, focus on your trunk and let the energies of the sun and Earth mix and marry in your heart and belly.

Part II: Meeting the Spirit of the Fire

- **Intention:** To connect with the guardian for the east of your personal medicine wheel.

- **Purpose:** To continue to build a strong sense of your own circle and connect to the resources that will support you as you continue your journey.

Now that you have been moving, have a sense of your relationship to the fire element and have taken steps to further embody this, it is time to meet the spirit of the fire in the dance.

Still moving, we invite you to look to the east and ask this spirit to come and dance with you in the east of your circle. As for your meeting with the spirit of the earth, trust the senses within you and focus your mind, your movement, your entire being on asking the spirit of the fire to show up in your circle today.

Be patient and feel your love for the living energy of the sun. Reach your hands out to the light and speak to the spirit of the fire from your heart. Dance with him and ask him to illuminate the way and to help you to grow stronger in body, heart and mind each day.

Feel free to ask him any questions you may have. What advice does the spirit of the fire have for you today?

Once you are done with your dance, thank him, release him and ask him to show up again when next you call him or in your dreams. It may be helpful to find an image or object, or make one, that reminds you of his presence.

Go and drink a glass of water and take a little time to focus on how this fire element might support you in your life. Fire gives us courage. Is there something you need to do, like write that letter, apply for that job or tell someone how much you care about them? Or maybe you just need to go and light a fire and sit with it again or lie in the sun and feel the nourishing strength of the light. You are as free and as creative as the fire itself. Enjoy.

Now we have visited the south and the east of our mandala, let's travel to the west and work with the water.

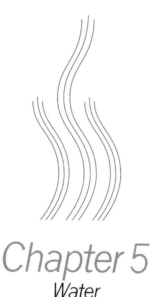

Chapter 5
Water

'We never know the worth of water until the well is dry.'

Thomas Fuller, Gnomologia, **1732**

Ya'Acov: *I was dancing in a circle of 140 people from many different nations at a sun dance in Arizona in 1992. We had spent a week together preparing the great circle. We each had our own small space and a lane in which we danced backwards and forwards towards the Tree of Life, a 200-ft tree at the centre of our circle. It was hot and windy in the desert and the conditions were perfect for dehydration. The sun dance goes on for three days and nights with only a two-hour break for dreaming between 2 a.m. and 4 a.m. By the time we had been dancing for 24 hours in the bright light and desert heat, I was feeling strange. I couldn't rest, I couldn't dance, I couldn't talk, I couldn't be silent. I went to the healing space and the healers took one look at me and told me: 'You're here to dance, not to die of dehydration. Go and take a drink of water.'*

Outside the main circle, a small water temple had been built. It was one of the most beautiful things I had ever seen. Flowers and images of Yemanjah, the Queen of the Ocean, crystals and beautiful carvings all held the space for a simple jug of water and a small goblet. Written in beautiful lettering were the instructions: 'Drink for your brothers and sisters who are now dying of thirst. Drink for your people. The water of life is sacred. Take it in and make your prayers.'

Trembling, I took the goblet and poured a tiny amount of the precious liquid into it. I offered it to the four directions and drank for those that couldn't. I am sure that more water left my body from my eyes than I took in through my mouth.

Drinking that small mouthful of water rejuvenated me. I felt life rushing back into my veins and I felt the force of a giant wave of energy building in me. I had to dance. I had to pray.

Water is the juice of life. The first life on Earth evolved in the primal soup of the waters. Before that there was no atmosphere to offer protection from the fierce strength of the sun's rays. The waters provided the protection and a context for the creative meeting of the sun, the Earth and the water itself. In the shelter of this womb, the first life evolved. Very gradually, enough oxygen was created by life forms to create the ozone layer. This provided protection from the sun's ultraviolet radiation, and life could eventually emerge from the waters.

Our watery genesis remains in evidence in modern life. In all plants and animals, life processes are carried out in the cells, which are full of cellular fluid. The network provided by water links and unites the whole body. It is the great communicator, the marketplace where action and exchange happen. Amazingly, water constitutes between 45 per cent and 75 per cent of our total human body weight – 75 per cent of lean muscle, 95 per cent of blood and 22 per cent of bone.

The water that comes out of your tap is a participant in a miraculous dance which has been going on for millennia. The molecules of water in your tea have probably been part of dinosaurs, been in the Ganges, may have been an iceberg, or a dewdrop on a lily in ancient Egypt. They may have been tears, blood, rivers or snow, huge trees and tiny creatures. Through all the kingdoms of this Earth, the perfectly balanced life cycle continues with water as a star player.

Water connects the whole planet, just as the water in the body unites our parts into one whole. It moves from rain to ground water, to streams and rivers and back to the sea. It evaporates to become clouds and then rains or snows back down in an eternal dance, always different, always bringing us all into one interconnected whole.

Creative Sexual Energy

Creative energy is sexual energy. And our sexual energy can be used in myriad ways, not just for making babies. Any creative project becomes illuminated with Eros when the magic kicks in, whether it's cooking a meal, dancing, making music or making love.

Your sexual energy is a magnificent and divine gift from the Creator. Sadly, within western culture our relationship with our sexuality has become distorted. We see this in the brave souls who are now finding the courage to speak about the suffering they experienced as children at the hands of adults who were supposed to be their carers and protectors. The statistics are shocking: one in four girls and one in six boys are sexually abused before the age of 18. Sexual abuse can lead to great loss of self-esteem, guilt, depression and even suicide. If we think of our sexuality as a beautiful river, the very lifeblood that runs through the centre of our lives, carrying our potential to create, we can see that in our society the river has become polluted.

So where can we go to purify the waters in us and plug into the enormous creative force of the water? We know of two places. One is to go the water itself. And the other is to go to the dance.

Water Ritual

- **Intention:** To give thanks to the water and ask it to be the next teacher, guide and inspiration on your spiritual journey.

- **Purpose:** To study the great shape-shifter and learn about the healing power of water and its ability to support us in following the flow, letting go and purifying.

If all that we manage to encourage you to do through this book is get out into some beautiful places to enjoy nature, we'll be happy. Here's another excuse to get out: we're inviting you to find a river. And whilst you're there, why not add in a little water ceremony?

Before you leave home, take some time to meditate on your own sexual history. Ask yourself, 'How is the water in me? How free and clear is my sexual energy? Is there anything that needs purification or forgiveness?' Make a list and take it with you. Time to go to the river.

Find somewhere by a river which is clean, safe and secluded enough to dip in. You may need to make a special trip to the wilds. Alternatively, you can adapt the recipe for the shower in your bathroom at home. Water is water!

Ask the water, specifically this river, to be your teacher and guide and to help you to purify and honour the innocence of your creative sexual energy. Spend some time simply relaxing, breathing deeply and watching the river dance. Open your awareness to enjoy the song of the river and the nature that is fed by it. Let yourself feel how each water droplet is carried by the river on its inevitable journey back to the great ocean. Sense how the river is held by the banks, just as the waters within you are contained by the structures of your body. Feel the life force in the river. Breathe it in. Sometimes the river makes us laugh with its playful unpredictability. Sometimes, it makes us cry, we know not why.

Once you feel you have made a connection with the river, start to tell it about your sexual history and your sexual energy. Ask it to carry your words and your feelings back to the ocean. Ask it to purify your body, your heart and your mind. Imagine that your words are like rain falling into the river and being carried to the ocean. Keep telling your stories until you are done.

If the current is not too strong and the temperature not too cold, now would be a good time to get in. Ask the river to help you to let go of some of the weight of your personal history and to wash through every cell and fibre of your being, bringing fresh life. Feel the water washing over you, washing through you. If the current is too fast or the water too cold, be content with simply washing your hands and face.

Now, find an incantation that affirms the purity, innocence and creative power of your sexual energy, something like:

'My sexual energy is a divine gift given to me by the Creator for my wellbeing, health and creativity. From now on, I choose to honour, learn from and develop this gift in a way which is in alignment with my highest purpose. I seek and I give thanks for the possibility of forgiveness for anything from my past that remains unfinished. I give thanks to the water of life and to this place.'

Once you have finished, relax and enjoy being in that place. Before you leave, make an offering of a dance, a song or a prayer and clean up any rubbish you found there to express your thanks.

Having learned from the infinite creativity and shape-shifting ability of the water in nature, we are now going to get down and get those life juices flowing inside the dance. Like water itself, your dance may take many shapes.

Water Dancing

Water is the great inner shape-shifter or alchemist which can transform itself in the creative cauldron. In nature, it surrenders to whatever form is necessary. It moves in so many different styles and is a master of them all. It can be a racing river, a delicate fountain, a sharp shining icicle, gentle tears, frost fronds, a plunging waterfall or steam rising from the rainforest. To sustain healthy life, it needs to change form and move through its cycle. If it gets stuck, it goes stagnant. Once it can move, it can cleanse and purify itself.

In all its different forms, water is still itself. When we dance with the water element, we invoke the capacity to be true to ourselves as we shape-shift. So we enter the work of transformation, where we can surrender to what is and discover more of who we can become. A caterpillar in transit to a butterfly creates a cocoon in which to dissolve. In the liquid, the building blocks of life are rearranged into a butterfly, which emerges eventually, wet, to dry its wings and fly.

In the dance, we invoke the life-giving flow of clean, clear water and we invite our polarities to meet in this fluid ocean of being in ecstatic communion. Such communion, whether it happens between lovers, or on the dance floor, or through a moment of pure awakening to the vibrant beauty of life, is most often a wet affair. Laughing or weeping or in orgasm, we come to the Creator wet as the moment we were born.

And when sensual earth and sexy fire become one in the waters of union, it is love that is born.

Susannah: *Sometimes the door opens and life is revealed in all its fresh innocence and indomitable, almost unbearable beauty. Here also is the suffering, the great pain that is endured on Earth. And holding and including it all is the love, the love beyond understanding. And I weep great rivers of tears for all the pain, for the beauty, the love and the holiness of life. Every cell is touched. The tears are a sacrament, a big 'I do' to life and love. And when the weeping is done, all that remains is to sing and to dance.*

These moments of recognition water the rest of our lives. We need these watering holes to remind us to look behind the apparently mundane and reconnect to the extraordinary gift of life.

We call this dance *Fusion*. Let's dance!

Water Dance

Part I: Fusion

- *Intention:* To experience the water dance and the meeting of earth and fire.

- *Purpose:* To connect with the inner marriage and the purifying power of water.

Take your space. Make sure you will not be disturbed. Prepare some appropriate music and make an altar which honours earth, fire and, centrally, water.

Start by calling your earth and fire guardians to be with you. Tune into the earth (use the *Earth Dancing* recipe if you want; page 00) and take some time to feel your weight and soften your body, letting your condition be. Acknowledge to yourself how you are, physically, emotionally and mentally. And let it all move.

Move with your mood, embrace it. Here is the Great Mother energy of acceptance. Let yourself be and slowly bring it all into circulation.

Then slowly invite the fire to come in. Feed that fire, give it breath! Feel your intention, your passion and the direction of your desire. Let it move through each part of your body. Remember that fire does not have to move strongly or in a big way, though it may. Ask the Great Father of the sun to shine on you and in you, and let the solar fire energy of the warrior in you draw a circle around your space, protecting you like the cocoon of a butterfly.

Now you've invoked earth and fire, it's time to add water and cook!

So invoke the waters – ask the water element to show you how to flow and let go. Let yourself shape-shift, following the water dancer in you, letting the earth and fire meet and marry in the water, letting all the ingredients mix and remix, sometimes finding patterns of repetition, sometimes letting go completely in your own fluid ever-changing calligraphy. Move between form and fluidity, inner and outer, and let the spirit of the dance take you and rearrange you. Ask for purification. Ask for cleansing. Imagine the waters pouring through you. Sometimes you come back to the earth for nourishment, sometimes you return to the fire for passion and heat, and then again and again you dive into your inner river, following it all the way to the sea, sometimes still, sometimes turbulent. And sometimes the shaking medicine comes. If you find yourself trembling, shaking or vibrating, let it come and let it go. This holy grace of transformation cannot be forced. Don't push, don't hold back, and when at last you are done, come to rest for a while before moving on to the second part.

Part II: Meeting the Spirit of the Water

- *Intention:* To connect with the guardian for the west of your personal medicine wheel.

- *Purpose:* Once again, to build a strong sense of your own circle and connect to the resources that will support you as you continue your journey.

Now that you have been moving and have a sense of your relationship to the water element, it is time to meet the spirit of the water in the dance. For us, the spirit of the water has many names. We call it the Great Shape-Shifter, the Great Purifier and, more recently through our work with our Brazilian friends, Yemanjah. As always, it is your own relationship to it that matters most. You are looking for a guardian who will have presence and personal meaning for you as you continue your journey.

We invite you to look to the west and pay your respects to the water. Ask a guardian spirit to come and dance with you in the west of your circle. Just as for your meeting with the spirits of the earth and the fire, focus your mind, your movement, your entire being on asking the spirit of the water to show up in your circle today. Be patient and feel within you your love for the living waters of life. Feel the waters within you and the amazing blessings that water brings. Dance with the spirit of the water.

Feel free to ask any questions you may have. What advice does the spirit of the water have for you today?

Once you are done, release the energy you called back to its freedom and ask it to show up again when next you call or in your dreams. Focus on the waters in you and the waters outside you in the world, breathing light into and through them, giving thanks for the wonder of water and finding a gesture to acknowledge yourself, your guardian and your new state. Bow to the earth, the fire and the water. It may be helpful to find an image or object, or make one, that reminds you of the presence of this guardian and place it next to your others.

Go and drink a glass of water with consciousness and gratitude, sending a prayer for all your relations and for those who are thirsty. Even better, find a project that helps people to create their own supplies of clean water and get involved, or give something, or throw a 'Celebrating our Clean Water' party to raise funds. Conscious giveaways are a traditional part of any ritual. They remind us that we are all connected and that we have a responsibility to each other.

You are three-quarters of the way to creating your own medicine wheel. It's time to complete the circle by finding your wings and learning how to fly with both feet on the ground.

Chapter 6
Air

'There are no limits to either time or distance, except as man himself may make them. I have but to touch the wind to know these things.'

Hal Borland

The air is powerful. We feel its presence as wind and as the breath of life in us. We cannot live without it and yet we cannot see it. So it is with the presence of spirit. The very word 'spirit' comes from the Latin *spirare*, meaning 'to breathe'.

The air moves across the face of the Earth. Of all the elements, it is the fastest and most pervasive. Like water, it knows no boundaries; it covers the entire Earth. The atmosphere reaches up 62 miles into space, though most of its gases are concentrated in the first few miles above the Earth, held there by the attraction of gravity. When you look at a bright sky, what you are seeing is the light of the sun reflecting from zillions of atmospheric gas molecules dancing in the light. The sky calls us to our heights, to fly into our dreams. Plants surge up into it, flowers shine, birds soar and play and flash. Stars sparkle through it, the moon gleams and the sun shines.

Along with water, air is the prime interconnector. And, as with the water, we have been polluting this source of life for a long time. We are now seeing the effects in the physical and spiritual health of people across the world. For instance, since the 1970s, in some parts of the UK, asthma rates have quadrupled amongst children.

We rarely pay attention to our breath and yet when we do, especially when we do something to deepen its sanctity, be it Movement Medicine, yoga or meditation, our life force begins to shine.

Susannah: *When I breathe with consciousness it can become so sensual, so blissful. The first time someone helped me feel my side ribs moving with the breath, rising and falling like wings, I felt I'd been waiting my whole life to feel that sensation. When I add my consciousness to the micro-vibration of my billion million cells, all breathing, I feel the light of the breath sparkling through my whole body, a full-body infusion of oxygen. It's happening all the time anyway, I just feel so different when I actually take time to feel it.*

And becoming aware of the spirit, similarly, how could I have forgotten? How could I have lived without the awareness of how the pure bright, luscious life of spirit infuses everything?

Shamanic Flight

'*We are the stars which sing. We sing with our light. We are the birds of fire, we fly over the sky. Our light is a voice. We make a road for the spirit to pass over.*'

Algonquin, *Song of the Stars*

Since the first humans walked the Earth, shamans have been travelling on the wind in ecstatic flight in search of visions to bring back to their people. They travel on the sound of the drum. They travel through their dance. They journey downwards or upwards through the roots and branches of the Tree of Life and into the lower and upper worlds. They do not fly for the sake of it, but for the transformation, healing or answers that their visions may bring. Then, like Father Christmas, they return through the smoke flap (chimney) of the lavo or tipi, bearing gifts for the tribe.

Worldwide, shamanic traditions, including ecstatic dance, have been misunderstood and ruthlessly attacked by missionary Christianity. Connection with nature spirits was long considered pagan and the ecstatic states of the shaman were held to be delusional or plain madness. However, the last few decades have seen the return of a deep fascination with shamanic practices. As a culture, we have found that the latest gadget, however impressive, cannot compensate for a lack of connection with nature and, through that, ourselves. Our hunger for that connection has led us to seek out what we have lost.

We have been blessed to study with many great teachers from different traditions. We have always felt that the gifts that we received from Native American medicine or from the Amazon were given not so that we could play at being Native American shamans or Amazonian shamans but so that we could remember our connection to our own traditions. Holding a ceremonial pipe for a few years reminded us how to speak to the earth, the fire, the water and the wind as our friends, and how to pray. When we had remembered, we returned our pipes with great gratitude and respect. Throughout all of it, our greatest teacher has been the dance itself, specifically the visions and inspirations we have received through our trance journeys.

A Breath of
Fresh Air

Ya'Acov: *I was out on a vision quest again. At one point, I saw a fine young man playing the saxophone in my vision. Naturally, being a white westerner, I assumed it was about me, so on my return to the world of daily affairs, I duly bought myself a saxophone and had a few lessons. Unfortunately, my passion didn't last long and work took over and I let it go.*

Many years later, I returned home from working abroad. As I came into the house, there was our son standing tall and strong in the living room, playing his saxophone, and I was stunned to realize that the vision I had had those many years before had not been about me at all. It had been a vision of our son-to-be.

At that moment I realized how much I had bought into the culture of the individual – in other words, thinking that it was all about me! My work, my visions, my hopes, dreams and aspirations. Me, myself, my Royal I-Ness.

It is really good to find out who we are – not just good but absolutely necessary if we are to give all that we have inside us – but on that morning I understood that in ceremony we may see many things that are not directly to do with our lives but connected to the much broader picture of which we are all part.

Visions are wonderful things, but they rarely come with an instruction manual. What we see in a visionary state is, in a way, the spirit of an idea that is born as a possibility the moment we see it. To bring that possibility into physical reality is the magic we are here to learn and it is in dancing with the element of air that we become light enough to work with conscious intent. So it's time to go and meet the wind.

Calling the Wind

- **Intention:** To meet and give thanks to the wind and ask it to support you on your journey.

- **Purpose:** To take a little flight of the imagination over your life so that you can see the bigger picture.

Here we go on another trip into the big beyond. This time we're looking for a hillside, a mountainside or a temporarily vacated eagle's eyrie. The important thing here is the view and the quietness of the location. If you're going alone, make sure that you have the appropriate equipment for the terrain and let someone know where you're going and what time you intend to return. Ideally, you'll get there before sunrise, but if all this 'getting up early' thing is too much for you right now, don't worry.

Once you have found your al fresco room with a view and feel you have received permission to be there, create a space in which to work and get yourself present in body, heart and mind through your Movement Medicine practice or any other tool you have.

Sit down comfortably and allow yourself to quietly enjoy the place and the view. Breathe in the fresh air and relax. Call the wind out loud, with a song or a prayer, but be sure to ask it to be gentle. Ask it to blow through the cobwebs of your body/heart/mind and open up the power of your imagination. It's good to ask the birds, as the guardians of the wind, to come and support you too.

Take some time to feel the response of the wind. You may be surprised to find that it is quite a communicator!

Now close your eyes and look at the journey of your life so far. Let your mind wander over the important and meaningful events in any sequence.

As your mind travels, be sure to stay aware of your body too. An easy way to do this is to keep returning your focus to the physical sensations within your body or the feeling of physical contact between your body and the ground you're on.

Now open your eyes and look out over the scenery. Look up into the vast space of the sky and down onto the landscape. Imagine that you could superimpose the important events from your life, starting with your birth, onto that landscape.

Within your imagination, open your wings. Keeping your physical body anchored to the spot, let your mind soar on the wind with the birds. Now, when you look back at your life, things which at the time seemed just difficult or random may make sense as part of the jigsaw shaping who you are. As you look down over your life, imagine that it has all been perfectly choreographed to teach you all you need to know and to strengthen you for the challenges ahead.

What else can you see? Can you see the blueprint of your soul laid out in the landscape below? Remember the power that comes from accepting what is and intending to move towards what you may become. Feel the open space of the sky above you and the light that illuminates your journey. Focus for a while on the potential you have within you to take your life forward.

> Feel the huge space of the sky, the light of the sun and the moon and the stars shining above you, and feel them inviting you to grow. Relax your mind and open up to any inspirations that come to you.
>
> Once you feel complete, remember to thank the spirits of the place and make an offering for them. Dancing for them is a fine idea. It's also a good idea to write down what you have experienced. This begins the process of integration.

You are a being of light living inside a physical body. According to the new physics, your body is mostly empty space. Somewhere inside the mystery of that empty space is the blueprint of your soul. It's up to you to find it. The air element can help you. You were born to manifest the dreams you hold in your heart. There is only one of you in all of creation. With a little courage and determination, you will be able to find your dance and step by step, learn to fly with your feet on the ground.

Flying with your Feet on the Ground

Dancing with the air expands us. It opens our wings, expands our lungs, our perspective and our view of what may be possible in any given situation. Our noses get a scent of freedom and rise from the grindstone. It's as if our eyes open for the very first time.

When we are moving freely through the journey of the elements, when we move from the water to the air, we often fall into trance. Trance is not special. Nor is it anything to be afraid of. It simply means that we become fascinated with where we are, who we are and whom we are with. The fog of our daily affairs lifts for a while and we see the bigger picture, where everything is touched and moved by spirit. We see the light shining in everything and everyone and, looking in the mirror, we remember who we are, where we are from and what we are here for.

Air Dance

Part I: Flying with your Feet on the Ground

- **Intention:** To experience the lightness of air, spread your wings and fly.

- **Purpose:** To support your spirit–body connection.

Create a space in which to work and get yourself present in body, heart and mind through your Movement Medicine practice or any other tool you have.

Breathing deeply, feel the density of your body, the weight, and let it drop, through a soft jaw, dropped tailbone, soft knees. Move for a while with your heaviness. Allow yourself to feel gravity working on you. Through your feet, or whatever part of you is touching the ground, feel the connection between the earth of your body and the body of the Earth. Keep this connection to the ground throughout your dance.

Now sense how your skin is able to breathe, and through the whole surface of your skin imagine breathing clean air. Imagine the air scintillating with life, permeating your cells, your flesh, your bones, filling you with zinging alive space. Keep breathing and moving to open all the nooks and crevices of your body to this luminous breath. Then let yourself dance – light and free, small moves, big moves, spreading your wings and feeling the air with your wingtips, soaring over your life, riding the thermals. You do not have to jump – you can fly with your feet on the ground, and you can let them move too. Follow the energy of the light bright winds, whether gentle or powerful, and feel how they connect you with all other life, through the walls, over the hills and beyond. Sometimes fast music is good for this, sometimes gentle. Find what you need.

With this feeling of light airy space inside your body, you can consciously make room for new information from the blueprint of the soul. It's as if you've cleaned out a room for a guest, opened the windows, let in the light and the fresh air, and now you are ready to invite more of *yourself* in. The soul returns as light to the body, so call the light and let the dancer in you decode the messages contained in the light as movement.

Let your dance be simple, sometimes moving in patterns of repetition, sometimes fluid, free, ever changing. As you allow the natural creativity of the dancer, now freed by the wind, to take over, you will gently, step by step, find your way into the trance of the dance.

Sometimes images will come as you dance and sometimes words, helping you to consciously welcome your own light into the body. For instance: 'I welcome back the part of me that dares to fly high in search of soul. I welcome back the wings of my imagination. I am a being of light living in a body.' This is a receptive or yin way of dancing with the wind.

There are also times when you know exactly what you are dancing for. Maybe you are calling back a lost part of yourself (see the SEER ritual, pages 163–169) or maybe you want to embody a recent realization. If this is so for you today, welcome this more intentional or yang style of dancing with the wind and dance to call back this specific light into the body.

When you are done, come to stillness and take some good deep breaths, feeling your gratitude for the light of the air.

Part II: Meeting the Spirit of the Wind

- **Intention:** To connect with the guardian for the north.

- **Purpose:** To complete your own personal medicine wheel so that standing at the centre of your circle, you can move on to your journey through the 9 Gateways.

Now that you have been moving and have a sense of your relationship to the wind, it is time to turn to the north and invite the spirit of the wind into your circle.

Look to the north and pay your respects to the wind. Ask a guardian spirit to come and dance with you in the north of your circle. Focus your mind, your movement, your entire being, on asking the spirit of the wind to show up in your circle today. Be patient, and feel your love for the living breath of life. Feel the air and the breath within you and the life that the breath brings. Dance with the spirit of the wind.

Feel free to ask any questions you may have. What advice does the spirit of the wind have for you today?

Release the energy you called back to its freedom and ask it to show up again when next you call or in your dreams. Focus on the air within you and the air outside in the world. Breathe out a prayer for the purification of the air and find a gesture to acknowledge yourself, your guardian and your journey up to now. Touch the Earth, salute the sun, drink some water with a prayer of thanks and bow to the freedom of the air that connects us all. It may be helpful to find an image or object, or make one, that reminds you of the presence of this guardian and place it next to your others to complete your altar to the four elements.

It is a good idea to lie down for a few minutes after intensive movement practice and allow the medicine to sink into your bones. Once you have done this, make sure that you are grounded before getting on with your day.

Congratulations! You now have the bones of basic Movement Medicine practice and we are almost ready to begin our journey through the 9 Gateways. Before setting out, we would like to take a little time to make sure that we have everything with us that we may need. So we invite you to work with one more recipe to bring together and deepen all that you have discovered so far.

Chapter 7
The Four Elements Journey

'There are likewise three kinds of dancers: first, those who consider dancing as a sort of gymnastic drill, made up of impersonal and graceful arabesques; second, those who, by concentrating their minds, lead the body into the rhythm of a desired emotion, expressing a remembered feeling or experience. And finally, there are those who convert the body into a luminous fluidity, surrendering it to the inspiration of the soul.'

Isadora Duncan

Now that you have danced each of the elements and met their respective guardians separately, we want to invite you to put all this together into one journey. The process of dancing the elements one after another strengthens the awareness that you are dancing at the centre of your own mandala and gives you the opportunity to feel how the elements relate inside your dance. Apart from that, it's great fun, excellent exercise for body, heart and mind, and a classroom for self-awareness all rolled into one. We never tire of it!

And remember: 'Dance like nobody's watching.'

The Four Elements Movement Medicine Journey

- **Intention:** To get to know the dancer within you and your movement medicine toolkit a little better before your journey through the 9 Gateways of Movement Medicine.

- **Purpose:** To experience how the elements relate as a dance so that you have a simple and effective practice that you can return to whenever you need to.

This recipe is on our CD *Movement Medicine Meditations 1: For the Dance of Life.*

Before you begin, take a little time to read over the recipes for dancing the four elements to remind yourself of some of the work you have already done. Create a space in which to work and get yourself present in body, heart and mind through your Movement Medicine practice or any other tool you have. Ground yourself at the centre of your circle. If you have objects to represent the elements and the guardians, it is a good idea to place them in the directions. A bowl of earth, a lit candle, a bowl of water and a feather or some burning incense will suffice.

Face the south and visualize the element of earth and your guardian from that direction. Bow or make any other gesture of respect and ask the guardian to hold your circle strong. Repeat for the east, visualizing the element of fire and your guardian, the west for water and the north for air/wind.

Back at the centre of your wheel, with the elements and guardians around you, the sky above and the Earth below, feel the Tree of Life within you, the deep roots going down into the lower worlds, the strong and fluid trunk that supports the heart, and the branches that reach into the upper worlds. Take a moment to accept how you are. Take another moment to focus on your intention for your journey. Say this out loud and find a gesture to acknowledge it. Now you are ready to dance.

Begin with the earth, move on to the fire, continue with the water and then the wind. Remember the yin and yang in each element. Follow the natural flow of your energy as it rises and falls throughout the journey. Enjoy yourself and give the dancer in you full creative permission. Remember, that dancer is already free. So, take the journey, wherever it leads.

Dance for as long as you want to – 10 minutes or a couple of hours. When you feel complete, take some time to lie down, focus on your breath, take in the medicine of your dance and receive the 'echo' of your work. Writing down your experience or painting a picture to express it are other good ways to integrate it. Once you have finished, thank and release your guardians, acknowledge yourself and take the benefits of your movement practice into the rest of your life.

With your toolkit in hand, let's continue with the next part of our voyage.

Chapter 8
What are the 9 Gateways to Living the Dream?

In Movement Medicine we work with 9 Gateways to what we call 'a full-spectrum life'. Each of these gateways reflects an aspect of life that we must come to terms with, whether or not we are conscious of it. The 9 Gateways path brings these aspects into consciousness and gives us keys to awaken the creative power within us.

The 9 Gateways

The 9 Gateways are:

- Body
- Heart
- Mind

- Past
- Present
- Future
- Fulfilment
- Interconnection
- Realization.

They are a map for our times. As you move through them, you will find and ultimately embody and share the full expression of yourself as a human being. You will be invited to grow your soul and, through its expression, find your place in the greater circle to which we all belong.

We see the 9 Gateways not as a linear process but as a spiral journey. You will find that there are gateways and qualities where you are at home and have strong roots and others where your connection feels weaker. As your practice deepens, you will be able to identify these strengths and the as yet less developed parts of your potential. We suggest that when you find strength, you celebrate, and when you find 'weakness', you celebrate twice as much. You have found the source of so much possibility. The beauty of the 9 Gateways is that they illuminate new landscapes that offer an exciting opportunity to explore and grow.

Through the 9 Gateways, you can dance through layers of impossibility, fixed patterns and ideas of who you are to emerge, fresh, strengthened and renewed in the direct experience of the infinite possibility that is within you, able to participate fully in creation, knowing who you are and what you are here to give.

The Three Journeys

The 9 Gateways are divided into three journeys, each of which contains three gateways:

1. *The Journey of Empowerment* is an invitation to experience body, heart and mind as three aspects of your own inner unity.

2. *The Journey of Responsibility* is an invitation to come into conscious relationship with what has gone before, what is happening now and what will come in the future.

3. *Living the Dream* is a clarion call to bring your own medicine to Earth and share it in connection, in co-creativity, in alignment with your highest purpose and in ultimate recognition of the oneness of all life.

The three journeys represent three axes of direction and alignment:

1. *The Journey of Empowerment* takes you through the first three gateways, which are *Body*, *Heart* and *Mind*. It is the alignment of body, heart and mind that creates the presence, self-acceptance and personal power from which strong intention emerges.

   This journey awakens the vertical axis that moves from your roots into the sky and back again.

2. *The Journey of Responsibility* takes you through the fourth, fifth and sixth gateways, which are *Past*, *Present* and *Future*. Honouring the past and taking full responsibility for your

life in the present will help you to envision and co-create the future.

This journey awakens the horizontal axis that moves from your background (where you come from) through the present (anchored in the centre of your body) to your foreground (the direction you are moving in).

3. *Living the Dream* takes you through the seventh, eighth and ninth gateways, which are *Fulfilment, Interconnection* and *Realization*. Fulfilment means bringing the gifts you have into full manifestation. The direct experience of the interconnection of all of life results in the overwhelming wish to contribute everything you have in gratitude for life. And the realization of your true nature as a manifestation of Divine Love is perhaps the deepest experience you can have.

This journey awakens the lateral and ultimately circular or spherical axis – from finding fulfilment in your own circle to interconnecting with the wider circle and finally extending your perception of the circle to include everything and realizing the truth of our oneness.

Let's start out on our journey!

...•• Part II ••...

The Journey of Empowerment

Chapter 9
Introduction to the Journey of Empowerment

'He who works with his hands is a labourer. He who works with his hands and his head is a craftsman. He who works with his hands and his head and his heart is an artist.'

St Francis of Assisi

The first quest of the 9 Gateways is an invitation to awaken, integrate and align your body, heart and mind. If we think of our body centred in the belly, our heart beautifully held and shining out from our chest and our mind centred in our brain, then we can visualize a vertical alignment of the body, heart and mind centres. We call this the 'vertical axis'. Awakening this axis, engaging and connecting body, heart and mind, is the challenge of the Journey of Empowerment.

Kabbalists use the analogy of the three-plaited candle to represent the light of the soul. One of the plaits represents the body, another the heart and the third the mind. When these three are united, the light of the soul shines through.

This approach sees soulfulness not as something that comes from spirit, from 'outside', but as a challenge we are given to weave together these different aspects into one whole, one soul, which then naturally finds itself in communication and communion with the Great Spirit, by whatever name you wish to call it.

When we become conscious of the natural harmony and alignment of body, heart and mind, it is as if someone has switched on the luminosity of the soul. And how the mind can soar when the body dances and the heart opens.

Movement is good for us: our bodies are animal bodies which are perfectly designed to move. They need to move for our health and wellbeing on every level.

And we are designed to *feel*, to love. We share a beautiful and potent emotional heritage with the mammalian kingdom. Our hearts are designed to move within the whole spectrum of feeling. They are designed to connect us with each other.

And we are designed to move our minds, to *think*. The conceptual mind is a powerful instrument for which most of us do not have the instruction manual. So we operate in default mode, unconsciously selecting our experience to conform to our expectations. We think that this is reality. But learning how to work with the power of our mind can change the way we perceive and experience everything.

Aligning body, heart and mind is the key to your personal power. Power in itself is neutral, but we all know that power can corrupt. Power without consciousness easily becomes oppressive. Power without responsibility is a danger to itself and to the rest of the family of life on Earth.

So, in the quest for a balanced empowerment, one question is important: 'Why?' What do you want this empowerment for? If you have felt powerless during your life and come to realize that within you you have the key to become more powerful than the source of your oppression, you are faced with a choice. As Confucius said: 'Before you embark on a journey of revenge, dig two graves.' If you do not do your healing work first, then it is likely that you will end up as just another manifestation of the very thing that victimized you in the first place. There are countless examples on an individual and national level where the oppressed have ended up as the next generation of oppressors.

So before you continue, we suggest that you spend some time meditating on this question: 'Once you are aligned and at home in your personal power, to what purpose will you dedicate it?'

Let's begin.

Chapter 10
The First Gateway:
The Body

*'Our own physical body possesses a wisdom which we
who inhabit the body lack.'*

Henry Miller

The body is home for our consciousness and for the spirit.
Through it, we experience life. We see it as our 'allotment',
or plot of land, which is loaned to us by the Earth, before we
return it, enriched with our life experience, at the end of our
lives.

Over the years, we have come to recognize that the body itself
is completely at home on Earth. Although we may not be at
home in our body, for a whole variety of reasons, it has its own
divine intelligence. The heart, too, is totally at home in the
body and has its own divine intelligence. The same is true of
the mind, and the more you dance, the more you will discover
that the intelligence of the mind resides in the whole body, not
just the head.

Separation of Body and Spirit

One of the deep wounds of our culture is the broken relationship we have with our own bodies. The history of western thought has led us to separate spirit from Earth, as we have been told that our heavenly Father is way up in an unreachable, celestial paradise and the body and its desires are temptations which have to be overcome in order to gain eternal life. What a con trick! And what suffering these beliefs have caused. Spirituality was once reserved for the 'holy' who preached the dangers of sensuality, physicality and sexuality to the masses whilst, in many cases, indulging their every whim in private. In some cases, the Church even went as far as to attempt to ban dancing, as it was thought to lead ordinary people into lust and other such sinful activity.

This focus on subjugating the body's feelings and desires in order to perfect oneself continues with a twist in its tail in the modern era. Now we try to control our bodies in deference to a physical ideal rather than a spiritual one. We have become super-conscious of the image we present. Fashion dictates the 'right' shape for the season and since most of us don't walk round with an airbrush kit to erase our 'imperfections', we can't possibly live up to this idealized image. Obsessed as we are by the perfect body, the reality is that we have become even more *disembodied*. The body and its desires are still being controlled and are now being sacrificed on the altar of our self-image.

Self-consciousness about the body is not the same thing as consciousness within the body. To shift our awareness from being concerned about what we look like or what others may be thinking of us to inviting the dancer to show us, from the inside, how this body feels and moves today, is, for most of us, a radical meditation in itself.

Looking at our own experience and looking around us, we see that the way we treat our physical body is a mirror of the cultural belief system into which we have been born. What Carlos Castenada's Don Juan so elegantly called the 'modality of the time' has led us to ignore the subtle language of the body and only to listen when a crisis looms in the form of pain or disease. Movement Medicine gives us the experience and the tools to learn to listen.

Receptivity, Trauma and Sensuality

When you are comfortable in the body and treat it like your home, you have a quality of presence. There is somebody home. The heart has somewhere to be and the mind has somewhere to recline. You have the sensitivity to feel and receive life, as well as the strength to act. We often think of sensitivity as the opposite of strength. But think of an animal like a leopard or a horse. Both qualities are clearly present and necessary for survival.

When you meet someone who is at home in the receptivity as well as the strength of their own body, you know it. Whether you are dancing, talking, making music together or making love, you can feel that they are 'receiving' you. There is a quality of softness and life in their body. There is space for a real meeting and interplay between your energies.

This is in contrast to the way many of us have learned to treat our own and each other's bodies. When we have been treated mechanically, as a 'thing,' or when we've been hurt, we become numb in order to survive. It is a good thing that the psyche knows how to shut down sensitivity when it needs to. However, the patterns we use to survive often have a cost: they reduce our capacity for being alive, feeling pleasure and having empathy. They also have a tendency to be still running the show years after the danger is past.

Michael Neumann is a brilliant sports physiotherapist who has helped our bodies out of many tight corners. He says:

'The body has incredible capacity to deal with damage. If a part of the body is injured, the muscles around that part will go into spasm, creating a natural splint, like an interior plaster cast, which immobilises the injured part and protects it. Our bodies know how to do this naturally and immediately, but they do not always release the "splint" once the injury has healed. That area of the body can easily stay traumatised and static long after the original injury has been forgotten. This is where it needs help through stretching or massage to release it from its now outdated holding pattern. Unless the correct rehabilitation is given and the proprioceptive nervous system rebalanced, the body will remain vulnerable to future injury or recurrence of the original injury.'

As in the body, so in the psyche.

It is extraordinary how the body will adapt to survive. There are many ways of doing this. Some of us live as if we have left the body behind, existing in an in-between world where we remain safe but untouched by life. We appear to be present, but the drawbridge is firmly up. Nothing comes in and nothing comes out. Though we eat, we do not taste. Though we touch, we do not feel. Others compensate by overdoing things. It's as if the only way for these people to feel is to have the foot slammed down on the accelerator all the time, with no time to listen and breathe in.

The sad thing is that when the physical antennae and our natural responsiveness have been shut down, we miss out on so much pleasure, joy and sensual richness in life.

Movement Medicine for the Body

So, what to do when the wisdom of our psyche has shut down sensation in order to protect us from trauma? In order to feel secure enough to begin to listen to the body and create a healthy and happy relationship with it, we need a certain level of safety and support.

The body is the storehouse of our personal history. Everything that we have experienced is recorded there. Through sustained, conscious movement practice (as well as other modalities of healing) we can transform the weight of our personal history. Once 'digested' by the body, heart and mind, it can become the fabric of our own wisdom and the source of much that we have to offer.

Releasing the body from patterns and stories from the past is a sensitive business. Forcing open a door that's been closed for good reasons for a long time is not wise. Though you may get it open, it is likely that the moment you're not paying attention, it will slam shut again and possibly reinforce the original story that encouraged you to close it in the first place. Not a good outcome!

It is not enough just to say: 'Move, and all will be well!' We need consciousness coupled with movement, gentleness coupled with courage, so that what we do heals rather than re-traumatizes us. We need to integrate the three intelligences of the body, heart and mind. Because all are inextricably linked, changing any one of them changes the other two. As we expand our movement vocabulary, they all become freer.

> **Susannah:** *I was dancing, walking, running in the space. Every now and again, our teacher, Helen Poynor, would say a word or two which would ricochet straight into my body. And my body responded, changed, shifted, by-passing my need to understand. It was as if Helen and my body were having their own dialogue, to which my conceptual self was an amazed witness. Imagine riding a horse down a lane and passing someone who strikes up an animated conversation with your horse about things you'd never even thought of. It was like that.*
>
> *Helen said: 'Susannah, you're energetically way above the ground. Try walking as if you are an old-fashioned policeman wearing heavy boots.' I started to laugh, and then I started to experiment. Putting my heels down first, taking big, serious strides, I paced about the room. 'Yes,' she said, 'that's more on Earth.'*
>
> *I suddenly remembered being four years old and racing around the garden of my kindergarten in Nairobi and being told: 'Girls should run on their toes!' I hadn't remembered that since that day. And here I was, at the age of 30, putting my heels down like a cartoon policeman and feeling the ghostly power of those 26-year-old words fleeing my body. New words came: 'I am a woman and I am here on Earth.'*

Later, as we sat down to talk, Helen brought my attention to the way I was holding myself 'up' and arching my spine. Relaxing my lower back and letting my spine soften and my tail drop, I burst into tears, feeling how I had been habitually holding myself up off the ground for so long. What a relief to drop down into myself and let my consciousness be held within my body and its connection with the Earth.

Fifteen years later, I'm still on a journey with this process of incarnation. Inhabiting the body can feel scary. It means a real commitment to being here.

As well as making that commitment, we need to be willing to start with what we have, to move small as well as big, and with an awareness that matches our dynamism.

Susannah: *Many years ago I was hitching in Greece with my lovely Irish boyfriend. One hot dusty day, with no cars on the road, we went into a half-built empty house which offered some shelter. I wanted to see if we could have lunch on the roof and raced up the stairs. I was really strong, and going fast, and I hit the ceiling very hard. I knocked myself out and came to with a neck buttressed stiff as a tree trunk. Hitching was strange, as I had to turn my whole body when I turned around to put my thumb out.*

A few days later, still totally stiff in the neck, I was sitting in a campsite neighbour's car and as my boyfriend tried to find an English-speaking radio station, I did an experiment. Very, very slowly, I started to move my head within the tiny circumference inside the 'jam' in which movement was possible. Microscopic movement slowly gave way to slightly bigger movement. As we sat there for over an hour, I kept breathing and just skirting the edge of the movement which was possible, not pushing, just moving within the confines of ease. Slowly the area grew, until, to my great surprise, by the time we had given up on hearing news of the Falklands war, my neck was totally free and back to normal. Use what you have and it will grow!

Interoception

Hugo Critchley has discovered that there is a strong link between our level of inner physical sensory awareness, which he calls 'interoception' (interior perception), and our emotional awareness of ourselves and empathy for others. Apparently psychopaths tend to have very low interoception. The next recipe helps us grow our capacity for interoception, which is an excellent foundation for allowing our awareness to expand.

Listening to the Body in Movement

- **Intention:** To discover the 3 Ms: Micro, Medio and Macro levels of movement.

- **Purpose:** To link internal and external perception and action, and balance dynamic action with inner consciousness.

Create a space in which to work and get yourself present in body, heart and mind through your Movement Medicine practice or any other tool you have. Throughout the practice allow your breath to be as free and as deep as your body wants. Feel your whole body breathing and being nourished and cleansed by the breath.

Pay your respects to the elemental guardians.

Now, keeping your focus on the interior of your body, let the inner dance come through. Invite the interior of your body to melt into freedom and fluidity. Close your eyes if that helps, but make sure that you are aware of the space around you. See how small you can let the moves become and yet how alive and conscious. It's as if you amplify the consciousness of the movement as you let it become more and more minute. If someone were watching, they might not even be able to see that you are moving. We call this 'Micro' movement.

Now slowly let the movement grow, allowing your torso and limbs to move through the space around your body. Your eyes are open. You are occupying the physical space of your 'energetic cocoon'. We call this 'Medio' movement.

Let the movement grow even further. Extend yourself, stretch out. Feel the movement making waves in the space and the waves resonating right out, touching the walls and beyond. Dance with what you see and feel outside yourself. This is what we call 'Macro' movement.

Now the exciting part can begin. Follow yourself in and out through these three levels of movement. You might go up and down through your 3M gears really fast or you might spend much longer at one or all of the levels. Let the shifts be gradual, though the quality of the movement itself – gentle, strong, wild or delicate – is up to you. Don't push and don't hold back. Just go in and dance with your interior (Micro), then bring that out and really let it move within your own space or orbit (Medio) and then share it in dialogue with the world around you (Macro). In this way, through the endless creativity of the dancer inside your body, you can find the way to bring what is inside you into relationship with what is outside you and bring what is outside you into relationship with what is inside you.

We will finish with a very simple practice. Sit quietly and settle into your breath and body with your eyes closed. Then follow the flow of your attention in and out, simply opening and closing your eyes as your attention moves from the inside to the outside and back again. There is no right or wrong tempo, and your pace may change.

After a few minutes, come to rest with your eyes closed. Take a few breaths, thank and release your elemental guardians, thank your body and thank the spirit of the dance.

Loving the Body You're Living In

In most new age philosophy, the body again gets a raw deal. We hear time and time again that we are not our bodies. For a culture that is already virtually totally disembodied, this is not necessarily helpful. It is certainly true that our bodies are on loan, but whilst we have them, why not look after them and enjoy them? We've heard it said many times on our travels that there are high beings in the spirit world who admire and love all of us tremendously for consenting to be in a body and making the attempt to bring spirit into form. Not only that, but they also envy us the opportunity that having a body gives us to experience the sensuality of life in such a deep way.

It may be a big shift to start to pay attention to your body and to start to treat it, in all its imperfection, as a friend. But we live in times where big shifts in consciousness are exactly what we need. And challenging as it may be, the rewards to be gained from discovering the natural intelligence and energy of a dancing body are worth any amount of feeling self-conscious or clumsy as you begin.

Ya'Acov: *I wasn't a dancer – far from it. I loved the physical side of life, playing sport and working out, and I'd always had an adventurous spirit, but dance? Forget it. Dancing was something that had been confined to the odd drunken party at college. I knew how to push my body, but not how to listen to it.*

I met the dance at a workshop with Gabrielle Roth in 1988. I was hiding out in the corner, wondering what on Earth had led me into a room where I was expected to spend the next three days dancing. I danced like a gnome, all hunched up and curled in on myself. I felt terribly cumbersome and self-conscious. Gabrielle, elegantly fluid and dressed in black, slowly seduced us into a way of listening to our bodies so that they could begin to find the dance inside. I was astonished how much energy there was in there when I was able to follow the invitation and place my focus on the physical sensation of the body moving and breathing. The difference between that state of listening to and following the body and the self-conscious patterns of thought that I was used to when dancing in a public space was quite shocking. My body had a dancer inside just dying to move!

Finally, the dancer and the dance seemed to take over. My body, which only a few hours before had been a tense mass of self-conscious patterns, now seemed creative, poetic, mystical and a guide to heightened states of awareness I had only experienced before with the use of drugs. I danced, I sweated, I wrote and shared poetry, and I fell in and out of trance and forever in love with the dance.

If you were to buy a new car, you would make sure that you drove it with the right kind of fuel. Wouldn't you also make sure it had the right oil level and tyre pressure and was regularly serviced? Basic and regular maintenance is the key to years of happy driving. The same is true of the body. And since it's the only one you've got, a little extra love and attention wouldn't go amiss.

What Does your Body Love? What Does your Body Need?

- *Intention:* To honour the body as the temple for the spirit and to discover what kind of maintenance, care and attention it needs.

- *Purpose:* To gain an excellent loving relationship with your body.

Create a space in which to work and get yourself present in body, heart and mind through your Movement Medicine practice or any other tool you have. Call your elemental guardians so that you get a sense of standing grounded and balanced at the centre of your circle.

Make sure to give your body all the breath it needs to support it to move in the way it needs to.

Focus your mind on the sensations of your body breathing and moving. Let your mind travel through your whole body and, as you are moving, imagine that each part of the body has a voice and is able to communicate with you. Ask different places in the body, 'What do you love? What do you need for your happiness and good health?' You can be as detailed as you want and it's fine to take a few sessions to scan the entire body.

After each dialogue, write down the answers you hear or feel and then return to your dance. It really helps to keep the focus on the sensations of the body as you ask. The body can talk in images, words, movements and feelings.

Once you have completed your scan and have your answers, sit down quietly and read through the messages you have received from your body. Thank your body for speaking to you and congratulate yourself for listening.

Now comes the crunch. You have a communiqué from your body. You can put it in a drawer and forget about it, or you can make the commitment to spend some time giving your body what it loves and needs. The question is, will you? In any process of empowerment, it always comes down to this in the end. You may have a list of 20 wonderful things to do for your body. But you don't have to do all of them at once. Ask your body what the priority is. Then begin.

As always, once you're complete, thank and release your guardians.

Ultimately, this awareness of the embodied sparkle of life that the first gateway invites us to explore will enable us to treat all beings, including ourselves, with respect and reverence. It brings us deeply into our hearts, and that's where we're going next.

Chapter 11
The Second Gateway: The Heart

'The heart of a fool is in his mouth, but the mouth of a wise man is in his heart.'

Benjamin Franklin

The central gateway of the Journey of Empowerment is the heart. The heart is the alchemical alembic that contains the powerfully creative world of the emotions. When you have transformed the lead of your personal history into the pure gold of an open heart, it shines out into the space around you, illuminating the way forward. A conscious dancing heart gives you direction, connection and freedom. When the heart is free, you have the confidence to follow your instincts and take action to create your dreams.

We have spent nearly 20 years working with the dance of our emotions. What different creatures they are when they are given permission to move. Gabrielle Roth, to whom we were apprenticed for 18 years, created a simple, beautiful and elegant map of the heart. This map invites the dancer to take a journey through fear, anger, sadness, joy and compassion and has been the ground of many of our explorations in the realm of the heart. In our Movement Medicine work we have integrated our experience of working with Gabrielle's map with our other studies in the fields of Gestalt psychotherapy, shamanic healing, neuro-science and animal behaviour and 20 years of working with thousands of courageous seekers.

Ya'Acov: *Gabrielle's encouragement to feel emotion in the body and then let it dance was a revelation. I was freed to dance all the pent-up energy of a lifetime of misunderstood and misdirected feelings.*

We were in the middle of our training with Gabrielle at Grimstone Manor in Devon. We'd been dancing deep all day, working with the heart. It had been an amazing day and at the end of it several of us were hanging out in the jacuzzi, giving our muscles a well-earned soak. Out of the blue, my heart began to race and hurt. I felt that it was trying to get out of my body and the pain became quite intense. I was afraid that I was having a heart attack and I asked someone to find Gabrielle quickly. For me, this was a big drama, but when Gabrielle showed up, she took one look at me, sighed with the humour of someone who'd seen this a thousand times before, and said to me: 'Don't worry, Ya'Acov. It's just the pain of your heart opening.' And off she went.

She was right. Sometimes when a door has been closed for a while, the opening can hurt. Her words had the effect of calming me on the one hand and releasing a dam burst of tears on the other. My heart had just slipped out between the bars of my personal history.

A Shift of Power

'When the power of love overcomes the love of power, the world will know peace.'

Attributed to Jimi Hendrix

Listen! The heart of the world is speaking to us. It's telling us about the need for a quantum shift in terms of what guides the decisions in our lives. On both the individual and collective levels we need to include the connective wisdom of the heart alongside the individual wisdom of the head. This means including our love for the wider whole of which we are part alongside our love for ourselves and our families.

We have grown up in a culture increasingly dominated by multi-national corporations which demand continual growth, success and increased profit at all costs. This way of being encourages us to make decisions without including the wisdom of the heart. How many times have you heard 'This isn't personal, it's just business'? But this approach is now at odds with our very survival. Trading our emotional intelligence for short-term personal gain simply isn't sustainable. With our world in a perilous state, there is no longer any space for relationships without the intelligence of the heart.

A Culture of Fear

The problem is that by the time we have become adults, we have been taught to be afraid of the natural intelligence of our emotions. In British sign language the sign for feeling indicates the breastbone in a gesture which has the flavour of something hidden and secret. This is an amazing mirror of our culture. We hold ourselves in. The British stiff upper lip is famous. We try not to be angry: we curl our face into a smile and complain in private. We try not to be sad: 'Cheer up!' 'Have a nice cup of tea!' We try not to be pleased with ourselves: 'Pride comes before a fall.' We often behave as if *any* emotion is a curse to be controlled, understood or analyzed out of us, rather than a natural and sophisticated part of our functioning. We are scared that our emotions will drown us, take us over and lead us into making decisions that aren't 'rational'.

So we have learned many ways of ignoring the heart. We over-work and over-consume, whether it be drugs, alcohol, food, action or entertainment. And slowly, the natural movement of the heart becomes distorted. So we suffer, our families suffer, society suffers and the world suffers.

Equilibrium of the Heart

We all know that the journey of the heart can be quite a rollercoaster ride. Sometimes you just have to hold on, close your eyes and scream. When the Great Choreographer provides us with a life situation where emotion hits like a storm, we need to know where the ground is and how to stay connected to it. Fortunately, we have been designed, through millions of years of evolution, to do just that.

The heart sits, beautifully poised in the heart of the body, between the gut and the brain, the roots and the crown, bridging heaven and Earth. If, through movement or any other practice, your body has become more rooted, fluid and free, then your heart already has a great deal of support. If you are not grounded in the physical body, when strong emotions arise, your energy will rise up into the head. You may well then end up lying awake at night, lost in the labyrinth of trying to think your way out of feeling what you're feeling.

Let's go back to our tree friends again. Think about how a tree moves in a storm: *with* the storm. The dancer in you can show you how to move so that you will remain grounded in any situation that may arise. Not only that, but as you become more confident in your ability to dance your feelings, you will find that experiences which in the past would have been overwhelming are now well within your ability to learn from. And you may even enjoy the ride!

Ya'Acov: *The very first conversation that Susannah and I ever had was focused on the question: 'Is it possible to be completely committed in relationship and at the same time completely free?' The first few years of our relationship were a chaotic journey. We had to find out through direct experience that our theories about what was possible and the reality of what we were capable of emotionally were not one and the same thing. Over the years, the trust between us grew as we continued to dance our socks off and follow a ceremonial shamanic practice and I completely recapitulated my personal history. I was intent on healing the deep fear of being betrayed and abandoned.*

There came a time when, after a period of monogamy, we were experimenting again with a more open relationship. I was at home and Susannah was away teaching. Our agreement was to check in with each other if there was a possibility of one of us becoming sexually involved with someone else. Well, such a moment presented itself for Susannah. We had a very open-hearted and tender conversation over the phone and decided that it was OK to experiment and see how it would be. I set my intent very clearly. I didn't want to die without healing the gut-wrenching fear that arose like a green snake constricting my heart when I thought of Susannah being intimate with someone else. Here was an opportunity to heal.

I went to bed early and lay there feeling all those old demons beginning their predictable dance in my belly. The snake appeared and I started to feel that familiar restriction of breathing and that cold certainty of dread icing up my perception. I saw the crossroads. Here I was again, with the very same feeling that I had experienced countless times before. The difference this time was that I had chosen it. This was a confrontation.

I leaped out of bed and went to put on some music. I started to dance and, most importantly, found my feet. I felt the reassuring presence of the Great Mother beneath me and I practised the meditation I had taught so many times: 'My heart is at home in my body. My body is at home on Earth.' As I did so, I felt the fire of my intent rising. I danced, speaking to the frightened one inside me, saying, 'I will not abandon you. I am here. You are safe.' The more deeply I danced, the more space I felt in my chest. My heart was beginning to relax inside my dancing body and I found I could breathe deeply. I felt as though I was breaking an ancient spell. The dancer in me just took over and the more freely I moved, the more deeply I breathed, the more space I felt in my mind. I was able to witness the intensity of the fear inside me, feel it as energy, and grow in my dance until I was bigger than my fear. My heart popped open. At that moment, I felt so much love rushing through me – love for myself, love for Susannah, love for my Creator. I felt enormous gratitude that I felt so much trust in life and in Susannah that I could just let go. All the sweat and tears

*in the dance and nights of ceremony were paying off. I felt
freer than I had ever felt in my life.*

*When Susannah returned home, the love between us
deepened further and has continued to deepen through the
years.*

Being grounded in your heart is not just about your own
emotional intelligence. It is the basis of the strength you
need to be able to communicate from the heart in all your
relationships. It takes great faith in yourself to stand up and
stay true to who you are in this world. It takes even greater
strength to allow others to be who they are. This strength
comes from knowing your own heart.

A Well-Functioning Emotional Engine

The heart is the seat of passion. It is the engine of forward
motion. Our first teachers on the shamanic path, the Deer
Tribe, rightly described this high-energy motor of feelings as
'e-motion', standing for 'energy in motion'. Emotions are a
call to action. If the energy of the heart is in motion, we act
appropriately and potently, with a clear sense of direction,
connection and freedom.

Direction

As Damasio explains in *The Feeling of the Thing,* all decisions
are emotional. Every decision we make, including the most
seemingly rational, is guided by a feeling of what is the best
thing to do. Someone who has lost the ability to process
emotions through brain damage is not able to decide what to

do. Instead, they go round and round in circles, looking at all possible outcomes. They have lost the feeling of what is the best course to take. An integrated emotional life becomes a sophisticated inner guidance system and keeps us on the right path for our highest good.

Connection

We share with all mammals the deep bond between mother and infant offspring, and in common with other highly social mammals, such as horses and wolves, we need each other. We grow up in relationship. Indeed, without relationship our brains do not mature. Our wellbeing on every level is tied into the quality of relationships we have. And it is our emotions that make that connection.

Our emotions are also highly connected with our physical intelligence. In the last chapter we talked about interoception and how our internal physical sensory awareness is linked with our emotional awareness of ourselves and others. Far from being a selfish state, we could say that interoception is the ground for emotional intelligence and compassionate action. For when we are not awake to our own sensory and therefore emotional life, we will not be aware of that in others. Cut off from the capacity to feel what others feel, we will be able to harm. Waking up to our hearts is crucially important if we are, literally, to come to our senses about the way we treat each other and the world.

We communicate our emotional state through our movement, our posture, our tone of voice and our words. Potent communication happens when word and heart and deed are congruent. When this is combined with a willingness to see and feel another's point of view, communication can really go places.

In the Middle East, there is a group called Parents for Peace. It is made up of Palestinian and Israeli parents who share the common tragedy of having lost one or more of their children through the conflict. How they do it we do not know, but they choose to reach out through their grief, communicate and attempt to build a link of solidarity, saying to the politicians and military commanders: 'You will not take revenge and shed more blood in the name of our child.'

One way or another, whatever our experience has been, it is the heart that dares to be loyal to the greater good that will pave the way for peace.

Freedom

If we are not at home in our emotions, we have to limit our behaviour. If we are afraid of sadness, we won't risk love. If we are afraid of failure, we won't risk setting out to manifest a dream. If we are afraid of fear, we won't dare to grow.

Once we learn how to be aware of our feelings, to befriend them and work with them, we find a new sense of freedom. Then we do not need to be afraid of ourselves, our dreams or each other. We have the power to act with freedom.

Animal Medicine

'Known must your fear be before banish it you can.'

Master Yoda, *Star Wars*

One way to learn about the healthy functioning of feeling is to return to basics and learn about the emotional heritage we share with our animal brethren. In new age circles it is quite common for people to talk about letting go of all their fear. The 'No Fear' slogan that adorns the clothing of extreme sports enthusiasts is in common with this. This is a misunderstanding. As animal scientist Temple Grandin says, 'A wild animal without fear is a dead animal.' What is fear but a superb alert system? Think of a deer when it hears a twig crack in the forest – ears up, quiet, still, totally focused: 'What is it? Where is it? Should I run or freeze?'

When you feel fear, pay attention! The adrenaline of fear tells you that action is needed and it gives you the power of fight or flight. Adrenalized people can do *amazing* things, often well beyond their normal strength. We need to learn to use our fear, not be afraid of it. How refreshing that the British Olympic swimmer Rebecca Adlington so openly described how, before her final at the Beijing Olympics, she was so scared that she needed to lie down on the floor in order not to vomit. When her race began, she turned her fear into action and broke the field and the world record in an extraordinary swim.

Temple Grandin also tells us, as anyone who has worked with horses will recognize, how the fine-boned, flighty, hyper-sensitive Arabic horse is both much more frightened, but also much more curious, interested and intelligent than the big-boned bombproof steady friend you can take anywhere.

In natural horsemanship there is something called 'advance and retreat'. If you are riding a horse and you meet something unknown, like a pile of gravel on the road, the horse will probably want to stop to get a good look at it. In old-fashioned riding you were taught to threaten, push and kick it into action, making it more frightened of you than of the gravel. In this scenario you become a part of the horse's problem, and it can lead to a wildly scared horse in default fight-flight survival mode or a numb half-dead horse who survives life by becoming non-responsive. I guess you may resonate with one or other (or both) of these survival modes yourself.

If, on the other hand, when the horse sees the scary unknown thing and stops, you gently encourage it to go *backwards*, then you allow it to feel safe and you support movement rather than freezing. It's as if you are saying, 'It's OK, we can go back if we need to,' and then the horse is reassured and its own natural curiosity will start to bring it forward. As it approaches the gravel it will probably need to stop and go back again several times until it can eventually walk calmly by, give the gravel pile a sniff as it does so. A horse with this sort of rider will give everything and be amazingly courageous and generous. And the part of ourselves that is scared is, we think, rather like a horse. So if, when we come to our own personal edge, we encourage ourselves to back off, we will find that our natural curiosity and excitement about the new can revive once we have established enough calmness, safety and sense of choice.

Building New Brain

In our 'Movement Medicine for the Heart' workshops, we practise changing the associations we have with more 'difficult' emotional landscapes into empowering and pleasurable associations.

How do we do this? The same way young animals do, through play. We play through many scenarios, using a form of movement theatre. Using our imagination and calling on the resource of the instinctual animal within, both the prey animal and the predator, we build a new reserve of positive associations with our emotions. We find that fear can be exciting and empowering, raising our energy levels and capacity for action. We befriend our ferocity and the nobility of our power to defend and protect life – our own, others' and the Earth's. We befriend our desire, our aggression and our hunting instinct to go for it! We befriend our grief, and the love and connectedness that always go hand in hand with it. We befriend our celebration and our exultation. We say 'yes' to all four chambers of the heart and our wisdom grows.

Through this process of building new associations, we are building new brain – literally, new neuron connections. As we make these new connections, whatever 'old' or buried emotion is ready to come out of the storehouse of emotional memory and stream through us in movement is welcome.

It's such a relief to befriend the full spectrum of our hearts. It means we can use our energy to live, rather than to keep parts of ourselves hidden, even from ourselves.

Susannah: *I was 19 and I was hitching across Belgium on the way to Germany to see my boyfriend. I'd got a lift with an Italian lorry driver. We'd shared our sandwiches and had a friendly repartee going. Driving through the night, he invited me to lie down on the bunk. I did, but felt very alert and wary. I kept my boots on and my eyes open.*

Then we stopped in a deserted lay-by. Still innocent, I asked: 'Why are we stopping here?' A few moments later he was on top of me on the bunk, trying to kiss me, his hand trying to wriggle up under my blouse. 'Uh oh,' I said to myself, 'this is it!' I saw how easy it would be to freeze and be raped. Or I could do something! At this point I heard my Irish kung fu teacher's voice in my head; 'What do you feel? Shout it!' A huge shout erupted out of me: 'No!' I bellowed.

Quick as anything he was off me, shouting, 'Aus, aus!'

I was out like a shot and then realized that my rucksack was in the back of the lorry. Earlier on I had felt so trusting, I had let myself be separated from it. 'Mein Rucksack, mein Rucksack!' I called.

He started the engine.

I wasn't going to lose my rucksack! I went and sat on the road in front of the truck. 'Mein Rucksack!' I shouted.

He got out, dumped the rucksack over the side and drove off.

Shaking like a leaf, I went and put up my tent under the trees, glad that with a tent, you never know if there is a young scared maiden inside or a paratrooper with three Alsatian dogs.

The next day dawned and I finished my journey with several easy rides, very relieved to be safe. I was so grateful for the kung fu classes I had taken in Dublin, through which I had befriended the power of my own explosive energy.

This story illustrates the purpose of practice and the power of clear communication. It wasn't kung fu technique that was the key. It was the capacity to let through the raw vocal energy of self-defence.

If we have been through trauma, or been frozen by fear or overwhelmed by emotions too difficult to express at any time in our lives, we need a safe space in which to play and slowly and gently create a new databank of possibility. Then, when we are faced with a situation in 'real life', we have a repertoire of pre-practised embodied possibilities at hand. The meditations in this chapter will give you a way to do this for yourself.

The Four Chambers of the Heart

Your heart is an extraordinary miracle. It pumps the blood through 60,000 miles of blood vessels and capillaries at a rate of more than 100 gallons every hour. It beats around 100,000 times a day and more than 40 million times a year, and it has an electromagnetic field that is 5,000 times greater than that of the brain.* And physical as all that is, it is the seat of an amazing force of perception called love. And all this in an organ so small that it will fit in the palm of your hand. Amazing grace!

In the dance of the heart, we ask for the support of the elements and animal allies to help us to find the energy and the courage to dance what needs to be danced. The animal helpers we use are personal to us. They each hold certain qualities that we have found supportive in the dance. If they don't work for you, please feel free to substitute ones that do. After all, it's your heart, your dance and your journey.

We see the four chambers of the heart as a mandala within the body. Metaphorically, these chambers circle a central courtyard. In the heart of hearts, at the centre of this courtyard, there sits your own inner archetypal wise man or woman, waiting for you to show up so that they can share the secrets of the power of love with you. This power is the greatest power in all the world.

The four chambers also relate to the four elements:

- The first chamber is the domain of awakening, where, supported by the stability of the earth element, we dance with our fear and transform it into the power of awake, sensitive alertness. The symbol we use for this is the deer with its ears pricked, listening intently, gathering the information to act from pure instinct in an instant.

Source: Miranda Tuffnell and Chris Crickmay, *A Widening Field: Journeys in Body and Imagination*, Dance Books Ltd, 2003

- The second chamber, illuminated and warmed by the light of the fire, is the domain of integrity, where we dance with our desires and with the power to protect that which we love. Our symbol for this is the jaguar, unequivocally protecting what it loves when needs must and hunting the object of desire with laser-sharp intent.

- In the third chamber, in the domain of surrender, the water dances us through our sadness and losses over the edge of the waterfall of forgiveness and returns us to the great ocean in the tender, wild and beautiful dance of grief. Our symbol for this chamber is the salmon who, in ancient druidic tradition, swims in the pool of wisdom, surrounded by nine hazel trees.

- The fourth chamber is the domain of gratitude where, uplifted by the warm winds of contentment and the breath of possibility, we fly with the hummingbird.

- In the centre, in the domain of grace, we dance with the wise elder of the heart who sits in truth and compassion, waiting for us to take the journey and join them there in the silent embrace of love.

If you work with all these chambers and the elder at the centre, you will, in time, create a beautiful garden of compassion for yourself and for all beings. Compassion is the source of the force of healing that is so desperately needed in our world and, whether you know it or not, you are a channel for that force.

The Dance of the Four Chambers of the Heart

Part I: The Dance of E-Motion

- **Intention:** To travel through the domains of the heart.

- **Purpose:** To develop the capacity to witness your heart and those of others with compassion and love.

Create a space in which to work and get yourself present in body, heart and mind through your Movement Medicine practice or any other tool you have. State your intention to journey through the chambers of the heart and ask for all the help you feel you will need. Your animal instincts are required here. Find and stay in your ground. If you can't dance it, you're moving too fast. Slow down and step back.

Visualize your heart in your body and sense how your whole body supports it. Plant your feet and let your heart receive this support. Breathing deeply, visualize the four chambers of the heart around a central courtyard where the wise elder of your heart is waiting for you.

Let's begin with the first chamber and the domain of awakening. Connect with the earth element and then call to the deer. Keeping your body in movement, ask the dancer in you to find the dance of the deer so that you can experience directly the alertness and the readiness for action that fear brings. You are the prey and you need your instincts to survive. Remember that you are a dancer, rooted in your body, here in the present. You are not looking to reinforce old patterns or stories of fear, you are looking to find a new language so that fear is not freezing the body but moving it. The more creative you can be with the shapes of fear and the movements that come from them, the better. Play! And be sure to stay aware of your breath and the physical sensation of the body moving.

Dance in this domain for as long as you want to before moving to the second chamber and the domain of integrity. Now call the jaguar and the element of fire. First of all, play with the forward motion of hunting and desire. Secondly, find and dance the ferocity of your will to protect what is precious to you. Move back and forth between the dance of the hunter and the protector. What are you hungry for? What needs your protection, inside or out? If you can't help yourself growling, go for it and enjoy it!

Stay there as long as you wish to and then move into the third chamber and the domain of surrender. Call the salmon and the element of water and play with the many shapes and dances of letting go and grief. You don't have to make yourself sad. The invitation is to give the dancer in you permission to create new possibilities for this watery domain, so that when sadness arises in your life, you have a greatly expanded movement vocabulary. This in turn will give you a different relationship to sadness and grief. The dance of sadness can be beautiful. Like water itself, it can be many things, from a tender tear to a wild torrent.

When you are ready, enter the fourth chamber and the domain of gratitude. Call the wind and the hummingbird and let your heart fill with contentment for the good things in your life. Remember the 3 Ms (Micro, Medio and Macro) so that your dance can expand and contract as you hover with the poise and delight of the hummingbird, sharing the nectar of a happy heart.

Once you feel ready, step into the next part of this recipe.

Part II: Meeting the Wise Elder in the Heart

- **Intention:** To know your own heart better.

- **Purpose:** To discover the wisdom that is waiting for you there.

Sit at the centre of your circle and visualize the wise elder of your heart. As you come closer, you see their old wrinkled face. You sense their benevolence and wisdom.

The elder opens their arms and greets you warmly. You sit down with them. This compassionate elder knows the mysteries of love and of your heart. In the silence you feel your heart being received and welcomed.

The elder speaks to you about your heart. Feel free to ask any questions as you look together over your emotional life and your relationship to your heart. Together, you take stock of your life and your current situation. You feel bathed in the understanding, love and compassion in which the elder is holding you.

When your conversation comes to a natural end for now, you feel in your pocket and find that you have the perfect gift or offering to thank your wise elder for their help. You give it to them and, as you do, they slip a gift of their own into your hands. You receive it, even if you don't understand its significance now. Then, bowing deeply to each other, you take your leave and return.

Place your hands on your heart. Feel its pulse and take a few minutes to simply thank and smile at your loyal heart that beats more than 100,000 times every day. Release all your helpers and then take the time to write down your experiences.

Your heart and the emotions it feels are powerful allies on your journey. Be patient with learning how to use the energy of feeling in a positive way. When the heart is grounded in the body, you will be able to play much more with your emotions. And there is another intelligence we have been given that will help us to do just that: the intelligence of the mind. Guess what? That's where we're headed next.

Chapter 12
The Third Gateway:
The Mind

*'To see a world in a grain of sand
And heaven in a wild flower,
Hold infinity in the palm of your hand
And eternity in an hour.'*

William Blake

The mind is a beautiful and multi-faceted jewel. It has extraordinary multi-dimensional capacities to perceive life and participate in its creation. When connected to a conscious body and a conscious heart, it is a powerful tool both for directly experiencing life and for co-creating the life you dream of.

As a human being, you have a choice: you can keep your mind fixed on the thoughts you have learned to focus on or you can allow it to grow beyond its conditioning and habits and become free.

Just as your lungs expand and contract when you breathe, so your mind expands and contracts according to what you focus on. Our intention is to help you to expand your view. If your mind has been imprisoned in fixed patterns for a while, it can be a revelation when the doors open wide and the sunlight streams in.

The journey from being locked in a fixed perspective to a direct experience of the unity of all creation is a great adventure, and on the way the mind becomes a wonderful ally, allowing us to see beyond the end of our own noses.

Mind, Consciousness and the Brain

The question 'How does the nature of mind and consciousness relate to the brain?' is a very big one. It keeps lots of very bright minds busy and is the subject of many a huge tome. We are not going to try and resolve this major philosophical, mystical and scientific debate. For us, the mind is all forms of consciousness. And the brain seems to have a lot to do with our capacity for consciousness. So we talk about the brain and we talk about the mind, and though they are not the same thing we recognize that they are linked and that knowing something about how our brain works can help us to become the master of our own mind.

Filtering

In terms of normal day-to-day functioning, what we perceive is not the same as what is out there. The human brain is selective about what it allows into consciousness. As neuroscience study after study shows, though we have similar senses to other animals, our brains do more filtering of that sensory information before they allow us to be conscious of it. Daniel Simons, who is a visual cognition psychologist, did an experiment called 'Gorillas in our Midst' in which a woman dressed in a gorilla suit came on in the middle of a video of a basketball game and thumped her chest. Fifty per cent of the viewers, who had been asked to count the number of passes in the game, did not see her. She was not in the category of 'ball pass' and therefore they simply didn't notice her.

No one has yet come up with a totally convincing idea of why we have evolved like this. Our capacity to miss things which we were not expecting may give us the advantage of not being easily distracted or overwhelmed. But the price we pay is that we don't see what is there – we see what we expect to see. And this is true of all forms of perception.

Susannah: *Once we came back from a week's holiday in the Bavarian Alps in Germany and went to IKEA, where I had an ecstatic Swedish meatball moment in the café. While I was eating, I casually became aware that on all the tables around us people were chatting away in German. 'Oh, that's unusual,' I thought. Then I listened more closely and realized that they were speaking broad Bristolian English. After a week of the sound, rhythm and cadences of German, my brain had converted the sound and rhythm of English into the sound of German. I didn't think that was possible, but I heard it. How much of my experience is being synthesized into what I have become familiar with?*

The Power of Attention

Our thoughts and expectations are certainly responsible for how we perceive life and the possibilities available to us in any given situation. In our workshops, we teach that energy follows attention. Try it now. When you place your attention on any part of your body, you will feel energy gathering there. You may experience this as warmth or tingling. The same is true of your life. Wherever you put your attention, your energy will follow like a well-trained puppy. In every moment, you are choosing your perception of reality, and this will go a long way towards determining your experience of your life.

Ya'Acov: *On a recent trip to meet the Council of 13 Indigenous Grandmothers in South Dakota, I had an opportunity to practise what we preach. I made myself late for my flight by squeezing in just one more video interview for a film I was making and, as a result, at the time that I was supposed to be boarding my plane for home, I found myself locked up in the South Dakota State Penitentiary for speeding.*

Reflecting later on how I had got myself handcuffed in the back of a police car, I saw a deep pattern in my behaviour that was partly personal, partly familial and partly cultural. I saw that 'just getting one more thing done' was part of a hunger in me that had never really felt satisfied. No matter how much I achieved, that part of my psyche would never allow me to relax. More importantly, that way of being kept me attached to the 'rat race' and inevitably led to more unnecessary consumption. I resolved to heal that wound and my first decision was a pledge to slow down my driving and allow more time in my travel schedule. After all, a green travel policy and driving at 100 miles per hour in a heavy American sports car don't quite fit, do they?

That little change opened a new chapter for me. A low-level irritability that my family had suffered from over the years became much more visible to me, and the choice I was now able to make to take an extra breath meant that this way of being virtually disappeared from my life. Not surprisingly, I discovered that I was able to enjoy the level of work I chose to engage in in a far more spacious way.

We humans are meaning makers. The meaning I have chosen to give my life is that I am a dancer and I choose to dance with whatever the Great Choreographer chooses to place in front of me. No complaints, only gratitude and the possibility to learn and to make the very most of the situation I can. When I first started to tell myself this story about life, there were definitely times of rebellion within me as old stories tried to reassert their authority. But as time has gone on, situations that might have truly upset my apple cart in the past have become easier and easier to deal with. In the back of the state trooper's car, with my hands firmly handcuffed behind my back, it was definitely an act of will to say: 'Beloved Great Choreographer, thank you for this teaching. Thank you for this experience.' To be honest, I felt like screaming. But if ever there was an opportunity to test out the reality that thoughts and stories, alongside body postures, can keep us locked in the grips of old stories about reality, this was it. I couldn't do very much about my posture with my hands locked behind my back, but I started by focusing my breath and changing the thought pattern with a few incantations: 'Thank you for this moment and this opportunity to learn. I trust in the divine intelligence of life and I am here in order to illuminate something that is shrouded in shadow. Thank you for this experience.'

Well, it worked. Within two minutes, I had regained my sense of calm and equilibrium and I could sit back and enjoy the experience of incarceration whilst at the same time, looking for the chinks of light that would enable me to get home in time to teach. After a fierce beginning, the police officer calmed down too, I quietly kept my incantations going and a minor miracle happened when the bail officer, who wasn't due for three days, showed up and was extremely helpful in suggesting a way to get me on a plane home.

Self-Reinforcing Loops

Our predilection to perceive only what we expect and to focus on certain thoughts to the exclusion of others makes us go around in self-reinforcing loops. Realizing this can be disconcerting. On the other hand, it is liberating and exciting. 'Maybe, just maybe, I am not perceiving the whole truth' makes a huge difference. It opens up new possibilities for ourselves and our relationships.

The Story

In our work, we call the lens through which we each filter the world the 'story'. Your story is mostly an unconscious set of expectations and beliefs about who you are and what life is. It is the lens through which you filter and interpret the raw data of sensory input.

As we go through life, we create this lens in order to make meaning out of our experience. Brain research shows that experiences associated with high emotion, especially fear, are 'labelled' by the brain as being of prime importance. If the experience which created our 'story' was traumatic or life threatening, it will be associated with acute fear, and we are likely to hold onto our story tenaciously, feeling that it is the absolute truth. In addition to this, once we have become scared and defensive, for whatever reason, our brain activity becomes dominated by the flight-fight mode and we tend to perceive that which confirms our worst fears. If we act from this perception, a mountain can easily appear out of a molehill. In the realm of human relationships, our stories, especially the ones connected with fear, can thus become a key part of the seemingly mysterious escalations of conflicts between individuals, groups or nations.

Being stuck in your own story and having it reinforced over and over can make you feel like the victim of an unfair world. Have you noticed how hard it is to love someone who is sure that no one loves them? Or how hard it is to let love in when you are sure it isn't there?

> **Susannah:** *I once watched someone struggle with this. Her relationship had just ended and she was feeling bereft and rejected. In a dance class, every time the teacher said, 'Take a partner,' she kept her head down, eyes on the floor, and didn't see the dancers who were trying to get her attention and wanting to dance with her. She bravely danced by herself, not getting a glimmer of the many dance partners who came towards her and who eventually turned away, looking for someone who could see them. She completed the class in tears, feeling upset that she had been 'rejected again'. But who had been doing the rejecting? Her 'story' had obscured the chance for her to see the different reality around her.*

How many times a day does this sort of routine get played out in our world, and with what tragic consequences on so many levels?

Five Steps

To help you to become conscious of the process through which we self-reinforce, we have broken the process down into five steps:

1. Story
2. Perception
3. Experience
4. Action
5. Consequence.

Normally the consequence directly reinforces the story. So we go on believing that it *is* the nature of reality. Here's an example:

1. *Story:* Dogs are scary. They always attack me.
2. *Perception:* A dog runs towards me on the street. I perceive that it is attacking me.
3. *Experience:* I feel scared.
4. *Action:* I run away.
5. *Consequence:* The dog chases me.

It *is* possible that the dog was attacking you. But it is probable that, why ever it was running towards you in the first place, you excited it by running away and so it ran after you. Your perception, and ensuing actions, precipitated the very thing you were frightened of and thereby reinforced your story: '*You see, it's true! Dogs are scary!*'

It is not true to say that we create our own reality, a popular new age fantasy. It is much more accurate to say that we create *with* reality. We are responsible for our perception of what is going on, and everything which results from this – our postures, our feelings and our actions – helps to *co-create* the situation we are in.

So changing our perception is key. In any challenging situation, simply being aware that there might be a story operating creates the possibility of perceiving beyond it.

Susannah: *Once in ceremony in Peru, I had a real wish to see the light, to bathe in the light, to receive the light. And all I saw were the dead leaves, spiders and creepy-crawlies making up the composting layer of the forest. Oh dear! I so wanted to see the light, but it seemed that at that moment my job was to see the dead leaves and spiders. I asked if this vision was there for my highest good. The reply was that it was just life happening in the ground layer of the forest. I struggled with my pride and my desire. I was sure that the other people there were having an amazing time with magical visions. But I eventually surrendered to how it was and settled down to contemplate the spiders and the composting leaves.*

After a long while, I heard a voice. It said gently, 'If you want to see the light, look up!'

I found a tree trunk and followed it up with my inner eyes until I burst up through the tree canopy and was met by brilliant birds soaring in the azure of the open sky. 'Ah, Susannah,' they called, 'we've been waiting for you! What kept you so long?'

I realized that I had been caught in a story about life being done to me and my job being to surrender gracefully to it. But I am the chief architect of my experience. Choice is primary. Where I put my attention is vital. To see the light, look up!

Becoming Conscious

Becoming aware of our stories, and accepting and changing them where necessary, takes attention, humility and a sense of humour. A big dose of self-love doesn't go amiss either.

Every time, through grace or intention, that we get a chance to become conscious of our unconscious expectations is to be celebrated, even if what we see about ourselves is not so savoury.

Susannah: *In 1989 we were on the second leg of our 5 Rhythms teacher training with Gabrielle Roth at Grimstone Manor in Devon and I'd got myself into a hole. I was seeing the dregs of myself and it wasn't pretty. I wanted Gabrielle's love and attention and she only seemed to see Ya'Acov. I was jealous, needy and in pain. I was a soggy mess. Everything I could see about myself was humiliating and horrible. Every time I tried to speak to Gabrielle to ask for some help, she disappeared around a corner. Everyone else seemed to be having fun, but I was in a hell-hole I'd created all by myself, and I knew it.*

I did everything I could think of to help myself. I danced my heart out whilst the others were having lunch. I wrote poetry, I washed in the stream, asked the trees to help me and prayed for the Earth to give me strength. Nothing seemed to help.

After a couple of days of this purgatory, I gave up. Eating lunch alone on a bench outside, I decided simply to enjoy my food and the sun on my back, the capacity for which, thankfully, rarely deserts me. Then it happened – I got it. 'Yes, I am this soggy mess, but I am not just that. I am also a unique, beautiful soul.' Of course, Gabrielle had been talking about this all workshop. But, as we have found over and over again, there is a profound difference between knowing something in theory and realizing it in practice. Our teachers give us the tools, but when the moment of realization comes, we each have to experience it in our own way.

I was transformed. Suddenly I could accept my shadows with ease. Of course the issues didn't go away just like that. But I was able to see the parts of myself I was ashamed of within the context of discovering the beauty of my soul.

This is an important key when we have, like Paddington Bear, wallpapered ourselves into the room of self-despair. Acknowledging that maybe there is more to us than this particular story can be enough for us to lever open the door and see that there is a whole house beyond the room of the story and a whole world beyond that.

Tracking your Stories

So how can we recognize our own stories? Try this: when you are asked a question, catch your first thought. The truth of your ideas about things often streaks across your inner screen before being obscured by a more acceptable version. We are often our own biggest censors. We can hide quite effectively from ourselves, as well as from others. So learn to become a fast and benevolent tracker, catch that first thought before it is gone and then be very kind and gentle with yourself.

Once your psyche learns that it will not be punished for revealing its inner mysteries, it will yield them up more easily. Here is an opportunity to practise.

Who Do I Think I Am?

- *Intention:* To become conscious of my ideas about myself.

- *Purpose:* To begin to become conscious of my stories and thereby open to other possibilities.

Create a space in which to work and get yourself present in body, heart and mind through your Movement Medicine practice or any other tool you have. Set yourself up with a notebook and a timer. Divide a page vertically down the middle. Then ask yourself: 'What qualities do I recognize in myself?' Using the left-hand half of the page, write for five minutes, in list form, one quality per line, including both positive and negative, for example:

- 'I am generous.'

- 'I am stubborn.'

Then go back to the top and write the opposite quality down on the right-hand side of the page. So the above example would become:

- 'I am generous.'   'I am mean.'

- 'I am stubborn.'   'I am flexible.'

When the timer rings, ask yourself: 'What are the qualities I admire most in other people?' Write a list of these down the left-hand column for three minutes.

Then take three minutes to do the same with: 'What are the qualities I most dislike in other people?'

Now put in all the opposites in the right-hand column. You may get some repeats. That's fine.

Now consider *all* these, both left and right-hand columns, as aspects of yourself. This may be challenging. But if there is something in us, there will also be its apparent opposite. The qualities we admire or dislike in others, we admire or dislike because they resonate with us. They have something to do with us. Just consider the possibility that you are *all* this and much, much more.

Now underline the aspects you feel ready to own and can easily accept as parts of yourself. Consider the others as aspects in hiding.

Take your time to digest this and see if it feels right to broaden your palette of ideas about yourself. Acknowledging the capacity we all have for light and shadow paradoxically makes us less likely to act out our shadows. It helps us to expand our mind and see new possibilities.

An Open Mind and the Unknown

As we open to new possibilities, it can be helpful to understand that, at least in part, we are creatures of habit. Predictability is a potent lure. As Bert Hellinger, founder of the Family Constellations approach to healing, says, 'It is harder to change than to suffer.' The pull of the known, however painful it may be, can catch us by surprise. As we leave the shores of the known and embark on the journey of self-stewardship, the vast space of the sea is scary. Tolerating this requires us to remain grounded in our physical awareness. If you always know where your feet are, you won't get lost. And as your perspective broadens, you will see that your life has the meaning you choose to give it.

Imagine an apple with a bite taken out of it in the middle of a circle of people. Imagine two people sitting opposite each other. One can see the side of the apple that is whole. The other can see the side of the apple that has a bite taken out of it. They are arguing about whether the apple is half-eaten or untouched. They could argue for days, each passionately speaking from the limited truth of their perspective. If it really mattered to them, maybe the argument would turn aggressive, with each combatant enlisting the support of others. Before you know it, they would be at war. This is the fixed mind of an idealist or a fundamentalist. A dancer, on the other hand, will not sit still. They will get up, dance all around the circle and expand their view. They will see many different perspectives, including that of their brother or sister opposite them. If we were all to dance, wouldn't our world be a different place?

Changing our Minds

'The intuitive mind is a sacred gift and the rational mind is a faithful servant. We have created a society that honours the servant and has forgotten the gift.'

Albert Einstein

It takes a baby around a thousand repetitions to learn something as seemingly simple as putting a spoonful of food into its mouth. Our stories about life are also learned through repetition. Once they are set, they shift into the background and we operate them without conscious thought or awareness, as smoothly as putting a spoon in our mouth.

Neuro-scientists, rather unattractively, call the brain 'plastic'. This means that it changes and develops depending on what it experiences and what it focuses on. This is evidenced by, for example, the differences in the brains of long-term meditators. It is now known that neuro-genesis, or the creation of new neurons, continues through life. This is new research, but it is a fair assumption that these new neurons make connections which are useful and appropriate. And neuro-genesis increases after physical exercise! So it would appear that when you dance and consciously focus your thinking, you are quite literally changing your mind.

For many years, we used to suggest to our students that they should 'stop thinking' and just dance. It took us a long time to realize that this simply doesn't work. Whilst there are undoubtedly times in the dance when the mind expands beyond its normal thinking and into the great peace of open mind, our own practice led us to realize that in the meantime, it was much better to give the mind something useful to think about. Nowadays in the dance, we work with three methods to expand the mind that mirror the receptive, active and creative dance that runs through the core of Movement Medicine practice:

1. The first is to become a compassionately conscious tracker of how your thinking mind works.

2. The second is to change the way you use your mind: first by focusing on what is happening in the present moment through what we call the 'poetry of presence' and secondly to focus consciously on the life you want to co-create using embodied incantations (which we will come to later; *pages 209–211*).

3. The third is to find your way into the naturally expanded state of consciousness of wild mind or ecstatic trance that integrates and moves beyond the first two methods.

Free your Mind

'All human mind is free and wild and needs wild land, its objective correlative. Societies that cage the mind, removing it from wild land, imprisoning it with clocks and enclosure and routine, pettifogging it with paperwork in a dreary photocopied world, run the risk of creating dementia and misery. The human mind developed in wilderness and needs it still.'

Jay Griffiths in *Wild*

To let the mind be free and unbound is so important to our creativity. To free it, we need to give it time out of the enclosures of everyday thought. We need to let it dance wildly in the lands of imagination, poetry and the unknown.

In trance, we are able to move fluidly between the left and right halves of the brain and integrate their respective strengths. We are able to experience the multi-dimensional mind that can simultaneously hold the paradoxes of duality and oneness, individuality and unity, and the understanding that everything is perfect as it is and we must go on creating and evolving.

In left-brain consciousness, we are aware of ourselves as individuals dancing. As we move into right-brain consciousness, our sense of ourselves as separate individuals dissolves like sugar in tea and we become one with the spirit of the dance and all of creation. The times we spend in this non-dualistic experience give the rest of our life perspective. When we experience left- and right-brain consciousness as integrated, the autonomous individuality of the left brain serves the oneness bliss state of the right brain and vice versa. For the two of us, these experiences have become the rudder that steers our ship on the ocean of the great unknown.

We recently met a beautiful Australian Aboriginal medicine man called Uncle Bob Randall. He shared a meditation with us and asked us to share it with as many people as we could, so we've integrated it into the next recipe.

Expanding the Mind

- *Intention:* To invite your mind to experience its ability to expand and contract as naturally as opening and closing the front door of your house
- *Purpose:* To directly experience your connection to the bigger picture.

You can do this at night in bed. It's a lovely way to fall into sleep and into your dreams.

Lying on your back with your arms by your side and the palms of your hands facing up, give the weight of your body to the mattress and start to focus on your breath. Breathe deeply and slowly. Go through each part of your body, starting at the top and including your organs, saying, 'My face is relaxing. With this out-breath, my face is relaxed. My eyes are relaxing. With this out-breath, my eyes are relaxed,' and so on through your whole body. When your body is settled, you may already begin to get a sense of your perception expanding.

Next, focus on the room you are in. Imagine your close family and friends sitting in a circle and see yourself as part of the circle. Find your own words to say: 'I am part of this circle of friends and family. I am this circle.'

Sense the room you are in and say quietly to yourself: 'I sense this room. I am part of this environment and I allow my mind to expand into and past the four walls of this room.'

Imagine your favourite place in nature. See it in as much detail as you can. Use all your senses and find your own words to say: 'I sense with all my senses this beautiful nature. I sense the spirit of the Earth. I am the spirit of the Earth.'

Do the same with an image of a tree, a fire, water and a place where you can feel the wind.

Now sense the sky above you and focus your mind on these words: 'I feel the vast empty space of the sky. I breathe with the wind. I am this empty space.'

If at any time this sense of expansion and openness feels too much, wiggle your fingers and toes, ground yourself, using your physical body as an anchor, and stop for a while. Once you are feeling secure and comfortable, continue.

You can allow your mind to focus on anything as it expands – a mountain, the ocean, the ripples of a stone as it hits the surface of a lake or the music of the spheres.

Keep inviting your mind to expand until you have gone as far as your imagination will take you. Finally, focus on the love in your heart, your gratitude for your physical body, the freedom of your mind and the spirit that animates all things and, again finding your own words, say: 'I am the source of the love in my heart. I am one with the spirit of creation. I feel the Creator within me and I am one with the Creator. I offer my total self in gratitude for this life. I am the spirit of gratitude. My mind is free. My mind is one with body and heart. I am. I am. I am.'

Continue with this for as long as you want to and fall asleep in this expanded state of consciousness. If you fall asleep before you have completed it all, don't worry. Sleep well. Tomorrow is another adventure.

Congratulations! You have taken your first journey along the vertical axis of body, heart and mind and we are sure you have learned a lot. If you're anything like us, you will have become aware of how much there is to learn and how many possibilities and opportunities there are in these first three gateways. Take a deep breath before moving on. As Adrian Freedman, a musician friend of ours, sings: 'The Journey is long but the Spirit is strong.' So before we move on to the Journey of Responsibility, here is one more recipe to help you to integrate the work we've done together so far.

Walking Tall

- *Intention:* To connect heart, head and feet.

- *Purpose:* To experience the alignment of the vertical axis and to walk tall with your heart open and your feet firmly on the ground.

Next time you go for a walk in nature, as you walk, feel the sensations of your feet, in your shoes, touching the ground, and acknowledge and thank the Earth with each step. Let your awareness of your feet ground you in your body.

Expand your awareness to include the heart. Imagine your heart radiant and expanding in your chest. Send out love to all your relations. Let yourself feel gratitude for all the goodness in your life.

Then bring your awareness up to your head and imagine your mind shining and expanding out into a halo around your head. Acknowledge and send greetings to the sun, the moon and the stars.

Breathe, and imagine yourself breathing life, spaciousness and light through your mind.

Breathe, and imagine yourself breathing life, spaciousness and light through your heart.

Breathe, and imagine yourself breathing life, spaciousness and light through your feet.

Moving your awareness up and down through body, heart and mind and back again, walk tall and enjoy this vertical axis! If there is anything you want to acknowledge or intend, do so with your feet, with your heart and with your mind. Give thanks for this capacity to experience inhabiting a body, feeling life with a strong heart and expanding your mind.

.... Part III ....

The Journey of Responsibility

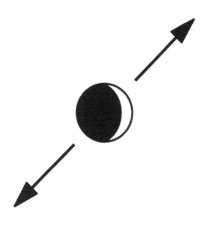

Chapter 13
Introduction to the Journey of Responsibility

*'I believe that we are solely responsible for our choices,
and we have to accept the consequences of every deed,
word, and thought throughout our lifetime.'*

Elisabeth Kübler-Ross

The second journey is central to our work together. This is both because it sits at the centre of our mandala and because it is the backbone of Movement Medicine work. We call the work with the past (fourth gateway), present (fifth gateway) and future (sixth gateway) the horizontal axis, or to give it its full name, the dorso-ventral horizontal axis. It is the line which connects the past (behind you) with the present (in your centre) and the future (in front of you). Awakening this axis, and taking responsibility for the full creative possibilities within it, is the challenge of the Journey of Responsibility.

On this journey, you will be given powerful and practical tools to transform the way you think and feel about your past. This will create the foundations to be able to live with acceptance, gratitude and purpose in the present, which in turn will determine to a large degree your ability to co-create a future that is in alignment with your dreams.

Not so long ago, we heard Tony Robbins, an extraordinary motivator of literally millions of people worldwide, saying on CD very clearly that 'Your past does not have to create your future.' We agree. However, it is our experience that what is unconscious and undigested from the past, whether it be our own personal stories or the stories that we inherit from our ancestors, our culture and the times we live in, will continue to have a massive impact on our experience of the present and therefore our ability to co-create the future. If that's bad news for you, don't worry: whatever your past has been, and whatever your situation is in the present, you have the capability to create with life. Over the past 20 years, we have worked with many thousands of people, some of who have survived concentration camps, torture and severe sexual abuse, as well as many of the less externally dramatic and more subtly disempowering experiences of growing up in the twentieth and twenty-first centuries. An amazing number of them have been able to transform their pasts from being a burden and a reason for remaining in victimhood to being a source of great inspiration for living lives of creativity, purpose and love.

The world is full of people who have refused to buckle under the pressure of their past experience and have gone on to make a positive difference in the lives of many people. We met one such woman many years ago, when she was in the last days of her remarkable life. We knew her as Grandmother Thunder and we honour her to this day. She had been in Bergen-Belsen concentration camp for several years during the Second World War. She came out as a teenager, having witnessed some of the horrors of what many people call 'the crime of the century'. Right there and then, she decided to dedicate her life to peace and to healing her experiences so as not to pass them on. Many years later, as a 70-year-old woman, having already become a healer of some renown, she went on a vision quest in wild mountainous terrain. When she'd been out for 24 hours and the weather had taken a turn for the worse, the organizers decided to send out support and a young German man volunteered to go. He was away for two days and when eventually he returned alongside Grandmother Thunder, everyone could see that something remarkable had happened. They were both radiant. It turned out that the young man was the grandson of the SS officer who had been in charge of the barracks in which Grandmother Thunder and her family had been held captive all those years before. She had been carrying the prayer to forgive her tormentors directly to complete her own healing journey. He had been carrying the awful guilt of being the descendant of people who had been responsible for atrocity upon atrocity. Together they had entered the cauldron of ceremony, shared grief, tears and remembrance and shared the mercy of forgiveness. This had strengthened them both.

Whatever our experiences have been, this story illustrates what is perhaps the most powerful medicine we possess: the medicine of forgiveness.

Eva Moses Kor, a survivor of Auschwitz (she and her sister were two of the twins in Dr Mengele's horrific experiments), talks about how, in her seventies, she arrived at the necessity to forgive, not for the sake of her persecutors, but because it was the way to let go of the victim role and to take back her power. She says: 'The power to forgive is yours. No one can give it to you and no one can take it away.'

You can do this too; indeed, we all need to find the way to make the past a support so as not to go on recreating it in an endless chain of action and reaction. We need to remember how to honour our ancestors whilst not carrying their grievances and sufferings. Why? It's simple. Our past creates the future, on a personal, relational and collective level, unless we choose to make it conscious and create with it. Just as a person who was abused as a child is likely to pass this abuse on in some way to the next generation unless they find their way to healing, so a nation that has been the victim of a nightmare in the past will become the persecutor in the present unless the wounds are illuminated, acknowledged, grieved and, most importantly, purified and released through the power of forgiveness.

A dynamic and creative relationship with the past and being as awake as we can in the present give us the capacity to co-create the future. The kind of intention work that we will share with you here acknowledges the interdependence of all life. So by 'co-create' we mean working with the creative powers of nature and spirit and the web of life and human community to support all life for the future as well as our needs in the present.

Now, having developed some sense of your personal power in the first three gateways' work, it's time to put it to use. You have it within you not just to heal the past but also to make use of it. This can give you the strength and compassion to awaken your dreams in the present. And a strong vision in the present can inspire you to co-create a future for all of our descendants and all our relations that is worthy of the name 'evolution'.

Chapter 14
The Fourth Gateway:
The Past

'Study the past if you would divine the future.'

Confucius

You have a past. It stretches back to your birth, your conception and way back through your parents, grandparents and all your ancestors to the first humans, back through the monkeys we evolved from, all the way back to the first life on Earth approximately four billion years ago. If you are alive, by definition you come from an unbroken line, four billion years long, of animals and humans who survived long enough to successfully pass on life. The echoes of the ages reverberate in you.

Roots

Knowing about our ancestors can give us a powerful sense of deep roots, one which goes back beyond the personalities of our families, reaching into the realms of myth and history. It can give us a new perspective on our own strengths and struggles. In our fast-forward world the past is often neglected. How many of us know the names of our great grandparents, let alone know anything significant about them? Most of us don't spend a lot of time honouring our ancestors or sending them a thank you in the form of a lit candle, a dancing prayer or a photograph up on the kitchen wall. Our lives are poorer without this kind of remembrance and sense of connection with where we come from. Roots are important. Strong roots make for a strong life.

The past itself lives on in us. We are the meeting of our ancestral threads; the ones we know about and the ones we don't. We are not merely burdened with our parents' crosses, our grandparents' losses, their grandparents' setbacks, reversals and disappointments. There are also gifts, strengths, achievements and wisdom in our backgrounds that benefit us, whether we know it or not. All these are threads weaving through the family soul, living on in us. We are our ancestors; their wounds and their blessings.

Susannah: *My grandmother, Maud Bruce, developed severe Alzheimer's as she grew old. She was cared for in a wonderful centre in Sheffield that specialized in the care of people with dementia. Her children and grandchildren visited regularly. In the last years she didn't recognize us. But I always felt she knew we were 'her' people. I used to get onto her bed with her and cuddle. Touch, stroking and physical presence were pleasures that remained available to her, along with the enjoyment of taste and food. Besides* *this, it was difficult to see what she was living for, yet she clung to life tenaciously, with amazing strength in her shrinking frame.*

One day my mother and I were visiting her together. She was restless and moaning, 'Oh, this is awful, this is terrible. I haven't done anything! Please help me!' We reminded her of the wonderful things she had done in her life, that she had been a great mother to four children and had been an inspirational schoolteacher and teacher of teachers. We said that now she could let other people hold the world and let herself be taken care of.

I don't know on what level she heard these words, but she quietened and became peaceful. Then she suddenly sprang bolt upright, said, 'I'm passing it to you!' and handed me something which felt like a symbolic torch, a flame. She and I were overwhelmed with feeling and as I sobbed, holding my grandmother, my mother came and put her angel arms around us both. I felt that my grandmother had given me the torch of her love for the world, passed down from her ancestors. I felt honoured and humbled and very glad that my mother, her daughter, was there too, blessing and witnessing this moment.

Some months later, my grandmother died as the bells were ringing at midnight on Christmas Eve, holding hands with two of her daughters, as the priest on the radio was saying the prayers for the dying. At her funeral, in keeping with Quaker tradition, people were invited to find their own words to celebrate her life and to commend her soul to God. One of her ex-colleagues at teacher training college said: 'To most teachers, students are either geese or swans, and they accept that this is the way things are. But to Maud, all her students were swans, and because she saw them like that, many of them became so.'

I was in bits. This was my grandmother; this was the woman who had handed her torch to me. I was, and am, am so proud to come from her lineage, so grateful for it, and at the same time sad that I had never known this about her whilst she was alive and that we had not had all the talks we could have had about teaching. And I was sad that she wasn't there to hear all the wonderful things which were said about her. It made me even more determined to celebrate people whilst they were alive, as well as to honour the dead.

Ya'Acov: *It's an amazing and sad fact that in the days that followed my dad's death at the young age of 53, I found out more about him than I knew about him whilst he was alive. His friends who visited to pay their respects told me all kinds of wild, funny and touching stories about him. It made me realize just how little we can know the people we grow up with and how multi-faceted each individual's life is.*

Ancestors

In the lives of many indigenous people, honouring the ancestors is seen as crucial to one's wellbeing. The ancestors are a benevolent resource for the living. For us, too, the past is peopled with our ancestors. Consider this: behind you are your parents, two people. Behind them are your grandparents, four people. Then eight great grandparents, and so on: 16, 32, 64... By the time we get to seven generations ago, there are 128 people. If we assume an average generation gap of 25 years, then by the time we get four centuries back, you have over 65,000 ancestors. No doubt some of them will be the same people, so the actual number will be considerably less than this, but it is still an awesome number of people, which just goes on expanding the deeper into time you go. Given the smaller population on Earth in past times, the inevitable conclusion, corroborated by genetic research, is that we are all highly related. Of course, if you go back to the first humans, it is clear that we are one family. And the further you go back, the more of life on Earth comes into that family, until, in terms of the common ancestors of both plant and animal life, all life is one family.

Susannah: *I was at Paignton Zoo with our son when he was a baby. We were watching the orang-utans, enjoying the little ones gambling and cute with their Charlie Chaplin quiffs, poignant eyes and gangly limbs. One of the babies climbed into his mother's arms and, right next to us on the other side of the glass, began to suckle. As he fed, he kept looking at us. Then our son grew restless. He was hungry too. I nursed him right there. Two mummies feeding their beautiful little babies inches apart. The orang-utan mother looked long into my eyes and then down at our son, then to her son, then back to me. I imagine she hadn't seen a human mother nursing her baby before. I wonder what she was thinking and feeling. For my part, we shared an eternal moment of fellow mother love and recognition of our familial closeness, separated by a glass screen. I remember her often.*

We come from our ancestors and their lives continue in us. On the cultural level, there is riveting research about how family patterns can recur from long-forgotten traumas from generations back. Until we have made conscious the patterns we inherit from our ancestors we are likely to be run by them. Assumptions about life may have come into being many generations past and still be in force today, often cramping our style long after the original story has been forgotten.

Susannah: *Many years ago I went to my supervisor with a query about my work. I had noticed that when I was teaching, my invitation to participants in my workshops to relax their faces and soften their jaws tended to become more of a command. I would go on and on about it. Of course, it does help the flow of energy if your jaw is relaxed – it's hard to let go into the dance with your mouth clamped shut! – but I was so compelled to get people to loosen their jaws that I suspected something else was going on in me.*

As we talked about it, I saw the mouths of my female ancestors all clamped shut. I saw their light and juice and voices hidden away, their energy dry and withheld. Dressed in black, pinched, bitter and resentful, they were behind me, holding me back, pulling me back. This was at the stage in my life when I could feel the music maker in me ready to step forward. But my ancestors seemed to say to me, 'No! You can't do what we couldn't do, we won't let you!'

Looking at them, I understood the fear that had distorted their souls. In the witch-burning centuries any woman who was a little different, loud, eccentric, outspoken, strong, sexy, disliked or a healer was vulnerable. No wonder our female ancestors kept their heads down and their light hidden and taught their daughters to do the same.

Understanding this helped, but still, what to do? As I stood at the head of my female ancestral train, the engine for this moment in time, I felt that I could honour their choices and the need for them, but that I would not be bound by them. Erupting from inside came a great irrepressible 'Yes!' to the life that wanted to stream through me. I stepped forward, and as I did so, a most remarkable and unexpected thing happened: the energy behind me changed. Like dominoes falling, the women came with me, not resentfully but with a tidal 'whoosh' of gladness and love. I felt a huge vibrant 'Yes!' from them: 'Do what we couldn't do! Take all this dammed-up energy and love and strength and juice and voice, and use it.'

My supervisor and I were blown away. I had had no idea of the power I had to change the ancestral picture. Soon after this, Party for God, my first album, came through the pipeline.

Our Stories

The patterns of the past continue in the present in the ways we habitually, think, feel and act. They are in our very cells. A German dancer and actor called Thomas Kampe put it like this: 'Whether we like history or not, it shapes and forms us. If I believe in something I believe in striving for the truth. It is true stories that count.'

Human beings are storytellers. We watch soaps, read novels, go to the movies. But in the modern world many of us have forgotten that we not only need to drink in other people's stories but to tell our own. In doing so you become a participant in the rich treasury of human stories; you add another dimension, another perspective.

Eva Chapman is a dear friend of ours. In an effort to make peace with her parents and her estranged family, she went on a quest to connect with what they had been through in the Russian revolution, the Stalinist repression in the Ukraine, the First and Second World Wars, and subsequent immigrant life in Australia. She recently wrote an extraordinary book called *Sasha and Olga* about this journey of healing. What she did not expect was how many people it would touch in a healing way. Many people have written to her in gratitude for telling their families' untold stories. Younger people have written to thank her for helping them understand their parents and grandparents. Others have thanked her for inspiring them to reconnect with estranged family members, recognizing the trauma that is often hidden under present-day conflicts. When we tell our stories, we do it for us all.

Susannah: *At home, in the kitchen where we eat, we have two 'family walls'. On one of them we have pictures of my parents and grandparents, and on the other Ya'Acov's, as far back as we have pictures. There are pictures of our parents on their wedding days, pictures of our mothers as children, a picture of Ya'Acov's grandfather as a serious young boy. There is a picture of me as a tiny baby with my mother, her mother and her grandmother; four generations of women beaming down on us.*

To begin with we did this because we wanted our son to grow up with a sense of where he came from on both sides, but we have found that these walls always fascinate our guests, and many hours have been spent with them, telling stories. Each morning when we walk in the forest and do our morning meditations, we thank our own and each other's ancestors for giving us the gift of life. And I have a sense of support at my back from my ancestry.

Making an Ancestors' Wall

- **Intention:** To honour where you come from in a practical way.

- **Purpose:** To nourish your roots.

Begin with talking with your family, if you can, especially the elders. Ask what you would like to know, but also ask what they would like to tell you. Talk with relatives you do not know so well, as well as those you see more often. Often people have information and stories that we don't know about because we have never asked. This process in itself can be healing and fruitful. Go gently and respectfully, with yourself and with your relatives if there are thorny issues in the way. Make photocopies of photos so that you can protect the originals and leave them with their owners.

When we did this we were struck by how little we actually knew, even about our parents' childhoods, how little we had ever asked. We found that this process was very moving in itself, both for our relatives and for us.

When you have collected any pictures you have of yourself as a child, your parents when they were younger or as children, your grandparents, and further back if you can, it's time to make your ancestors' wall. Framing the pictures, even in simple clip frames, gives them a nice sense of dignity. When you have them all ready, and have your wall clean and clear to receive them, you may want to put them up alone, or with friends or family. When they are all up, name all the people there. If there are people missing, it is good to acknowledge their existence, too, even if they have been forgotten or excluded. Light a candle for them all and find a way to thank them for enduring their trials, as they surely did, with all the dignity they could muster, and for giving you life, and maybe the chance to go further than they did.

If your relatives were involved in helping you find the pictures, you could have a 'wall warming' and invite everyone around for a little celebration. Don't be surprised if there are tensions – 'Uncle Ted shouldn't

> be there after what he did!' – but we would be
> surprised if, ultimately, your wall did not warm your
> family.
>
> If, for any reason, you don't have access to your
> immediate family, and don't have pictures, you might
> feel a loss at this lack. If so, you could make your
> own ceremony to acknowledge them. Write a letter to
> them and send it by 'spirit post' by reading it and then
> burning it ceremonially in the fire. Follow any leads
> you have, use any pictures you do have, draw your
> impressions of your ancestors.

If you decide that you want to find out more about where
you come from, there's no knowing what you might find. The
search can be surprising, illuminating, exhilarating and often
healing. It can also be a painful and painstaking process.
This is especially so if you don't know your roots. For those
of us who don't know one or other parent, or who have been
adopted, or have been in care, or had a rough or barren ride
with our parents, the question 'Where do I come from?' may
not have an easy answer. The search for roots and a sense
of belonging can be a lifelong one. But claiming our own
particular past, especially if we have been ashamed of it,
can be a redemptive act which gives roots to our lives now.
In this process, it's important to find the support we need to
acknowledge the pain, find the chinks of light within it and
become a witness rather than a victim of what happened. Our
losses can eventually become doorways to greater compassion
for ourselves and others and can help us find some meaning
in our experience.

Remember that, by definition, you come from an unbroken line of people, and further back, animals, all of whom survived long enough to successfully reproduce. So you come from strong ancestors! Whatever the trauma in your lineage, if you go back far enough there will be ancestors who were whole, healthy, vital and whose life force runs in you. You can connect with this and strengthen it with your gratitude and awareness if you choose to. And if you do the following recipe, you may find out you know more than you imagined.

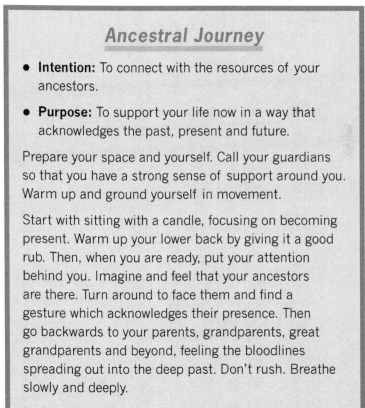

Ancestral Journey

- **Intention:** To connect with the resources of your ancestors.

- **Purpose:** To support your life now in a way that acknowledges the past, present and future.

Prepare your space and yourself. Call your guardians so that you have a strong sense of support around you. Warm up and ground yourself in movement.

Start with sitting with a candle, focusing on becoming present. Warm up your lower back by giving it a good rub. Then, when you are ready, put your attention behind you. Imagine and feel that your ancestors are there. Turn around to face them and find a gesture which acknowledges their presence. Then go backwards to your parents, grandparents, great grandparents and beyond, feeling the bloodlines spreading out into the deep past. Don't rush. Breathe slowly and deeply.

In the deep past, you see a candle or torch being carried by an ancestor. This is the flame of life. See it slowly being passed forwards generation by generation. Look at the images, landscapes and feelings it illuminates as it passes.

Once in a while, an ancestor steps forwards who loves you. You speak together. They have a message for you. Ask whatever questions you wish. Say whatever you want to say. If it's someone you knew in this life, take the time to see them as they are now. Don't hold them in the picture you have of them. You may be surprised to find out that they have gone on changing and growing. Before they return to their place in the web you realize you have a gift for them and they have one for you. Trust what comes. When you are ready, say goodbye, thank them and let them go back to their place in the web.

Finally, the flame of life is passed to you. Consciously receive it.

Find a gesture which acknowledges and thanks your ancestry for bringing you life and then turn to face your original direction. Feel the support of your ancestors behind you. Feel yourself in the present, in your body here and now, breathing into your belly, feeling your feet on the ground, the sun in your heart and your crown lifted towards the sky. Then become aware of the future in front of you. Offer those who will follow you a blessing from your place now.

You may want to write or draw or paint what you found on this journey. You might want to add anything you create to your family wall. This experience of doing this may be surprisingly emotional as well as strengthening. It can be a beautiful thing to share with a friend. Be gentle with yourself and do something to ground yourself.

So far in this chapter we have been looking at our ancestral past. Now we will shift the focus to taking responsibility for transforming our personal histories.

Soul Loss

When a new shoot pops out from the ground in the spring, it needs nourishment from the earth and the rain and the light of the sun in order to grow. We are the same. As children, when a new expression or quality arises in us, in an ideal world, our loving family would be as present as the sun and the earth to give us all we needed to grow with confidence. Unfortunately, since we live in times when most parents are busy rushing around trying to earn the money to pay the monthly bills, these subtle moments of growth get missed all the time. So sometimes the tender shoots are trampled underfoot and end up leading to destructive patterns of behaviour later on.

Imagine a little girl happily making a lovely mess in the kitchen and a father returning from a demanding day at work. The child is proud of her fairy feasts and wants to share the joy of her creation with her dear papa. Unfortunately, papa just wants to sit down, have a beer and watch TV. More than that, he's irritated by the mess in the kitchen and when his daughter runs up to him, he snaps at her and tells her to clean it up. If this happens once, she'll be a little upset but it will pass. However, if it becomes a pattern, there will be a moment when, in order to stop the pain of receiving her father's frustrations, she will simply stop showing him her day's creations. She may end up with the story that creativity doesn't get you the love and attention you need to grow – quite the opposite, in fact. Later in life, she will associate creativity with irritation and the withdrawal of love, and her precious creations may never see the light of day again.

In shamanic speak, the girl has lost the creative part of her soul. What shamans call 'soul loss' is where parts of us simply cannot cope with an experience and leave the body in order for us to survive. The mess in the kitchen is a simple example, but imagine more traumatic situations like violence or sexual abuse and you will start to see that these situations from the past can have a major impact on our lives.

The moment of soul loss, when a person, through the pure instinct of survival, makes a choice, is called an 'energetic command', a term we first heard from Victor Sanchez. It is possible to look back at hundreds of events in our lives and trace them back to one energetic command and one soul choice we made for our survival.

So where does the soul piece go when it leaves the body? One way of seeing it is that it goes to 'Soul School', continuing to evolve in an in-between world, waiting for the day when we are ready to receive it back again into the flow of our life.

And what does it feel like to have lost a part of the soul? Like that feeling you sometimes have when you're leaving somebody's house and you're sure you've left something behind. It's that feeling of incompleteness that our modern mass advertising industry speaks to so very well. Buying a product to make ourselves 'complete' gives us a satisfaction high, but it only lasts a short time and then we're left hungry again. The reason for this is that what's actually missing is our very own soul, and nothing else, no matter how sparkling or shiny, will fill that empty space. Nothing other than the retrieval of that lost piece of soul will give us the true and lasting happiness that comes from being who we are.

Ya'Acov: *In telling you this story, I want to let you know that I have no sense of blame any more. This event was part of my childhood. It became part of my psyche and I wouldn't, given the chance, change a single thing about what happened.*

I was seven years old and I had been invited to be a pageboy at a cousin's wedding. My mother had taken me to Manchester to buy my pageboy kit and we had ended up buying a beautiful dark blue velvet jacket. It had gone to the tailor for alteration and, as chance had it, it arrived back late one Friday afternoon. I loved it and couldn't wait to show my dad. But depending on the kind of week my dad had had, there was sometimes a lot of tension present at Friday dinner. And that week must have been tough. Dad had had an extra whisky. I could smell it on his breath.

We were eating dessert and my dad had drunk another whisky or two when my mum said: 'Go and get your jacket and show it to your dad.' I was so excited and happy, and I ran up the stairs two at a time, found the brown paper parcel wrapped in string, tore it open and put on my new shiny blue velvet jacket. I took a quick peep in the mirror, smiled at my reflection, raced down the stairs and presented myself to my dad. He took one look at me and then turned angrily to my mum. 'How much did that jacket cost?'

'Twenty pounds,' she replied. It was a lot of money in those days.

Without warning, my father swung round and slapped me hard across the face. I was stunned, stinging with humiliation and smarting with pain. I didn't say anything, but turned around quickly, desperate that he shouldn't see my tears, and raced back up to my bedroom, where I collapsed onto my bed.

For my dad, it was a moment of anger and a channel for frustration. It happened quickly and then it was over. I wasn't injured physically. My father was not in the habit of using physical violence, but for me something broke in that moment. My whole energy seemed to take on an 'I'll show you!' shape. My heart closed to my father and it took much suffering for us both before it opened up again. On the other hand, the 'I'll show you!' dance was certainly a source of much of the strength of will that served me so well in my adolescence and, now that it is no longer connected to a source of anger, continues to serve me now.

Children are generally much more sensitive than adults. Moments like that can stick with them for a long time. I managed to hold my father's fast-moving hand against the side of my face for over 15 years before I found the dance in which I was able to feel it, express it, let it go and find the teachings in it. Forgiveness then was easy, a putting down of a burden that I had carried for all that time.

Soul Retrieval

Healing is a process. Forgiveness is a key element in that process and comes naturally as part of that journey. Of course, in remembering something difficult that has happened to us, we may feel all kinds of emotions and all kinds of thoughts may arise. Blame and guilt are part of what we have learned. Our culture thrives on them. We learn pretty quickly that whatever happens, it is always someone's fault. Some of us have learned to assume that it is we who are guilty. Others habitually cast the blame outside ourselves. Sometimes these patterns of blame and guilt are carried across generations. But the blame–guilt dance is not good for the blamer *or* the blamed. It may well be part of our initial response to events, but it is no more than a dance that must pass through us and then be released.

As adults, with sufficient support and guidance, we can look at any situation from our past, including trauma and challenging times, and extract the maximum benefit from it. In so doing, we retrieve those parts of the soul that had to leave and come to benefit from all they have been learning for us in 'Soul School'.

> **Ya'Acov:** *One time in the dance, after my father had died, I found myself in trance and as well as being absolutely present in the room and in the beat, my spirit was journeying. I found myself in a forest on a horse, a warrior dressed for battle. I knew I was seeking something out. I cantered along the forest path, a sense of urgency driving me on. In the distance, in a clearing, I saw what I was looking for. There, standing under the protective shadow of a big oak in full leaf, was a child with two shadowy hooded figures behind him.*
>
> *Sword in hand, I prepared to do battle with these figures, who I was sure had kidnapped this young boy. I approached fast, and breathlessly shouted out: 'It's OK, I've come for you!' As I drew closer, I recognized the boy as the seven-year-old part of myself that had gone missing at the moment that my father's hand had hit my face so many years before.*
>
> *Deeply involved in the drama of rescue, I dismounted – and was stopped in my tracks by the sound of laughter. I looked up and saw to my amazement that the child was laughing at me. 'No,' he said, 'I've come for you.'*
>
> *It turned out that he'd been living with these two figures ever since he'd left and they had been teaching him all*

that I needed to know at that time. I thought I had come to rescue him, but in fact it was the other way round. As I took him into my arms, tears streaming, I took back into myself the quality of innocence and sheer delight in life that this child had held safe for me for all this time. I thanked his guardians, for that is what they were, and danced him all the way back home, right back into my muscles, into my bones, into the cellular structure of my body.

Later, in meditation, the child said to me: 'Thanks for doing the work to make space for me.' The work had been years of taking back possession of my own physical body, purifying, letting my heart dance and making space for this vital part of my own soul to return home.

Movement Medicine takes us, step by step, through the territories of the past, not to dwell there but to release that which no longer serves us and to call back that which we may have lost. Soul retrieval is the process by which we literally bring back to life the qualities we were born with. Over the years, we have developed simple techniques to help ourselves and our students do the work of retrieving lost and separated parts of our essential energy. Sometimes it happens spontaneously in the dance and other times we have found it necessary to go hunting. The most effective technique that we have developed that you can do for yourself is called 'the SEER process'. SEER stands for 'Systemic Essential Energy Retrieval'. It is a great tool for dealing with a difficult moment from your past – or even a difficult day that you have just had. It can take as little as 15 minutes to do it thoroughly and we and many of our students have found it very effective for releasing stress and shifting old patterns that seemed destined to stay stuck for ever. We're going to share it with you here, but we want to stress that it is important that you have enough internal support to be able to do this work. For deeply traumatized parts of the self, we recommend the presence of a good and well-qualified

therapist to support you through the healing work you may
need to do.

The SEER Process

- **Intention:** To release the effects of a difficult day,
  practise different options and retrieve parts of the
  soul that have been at 'Soul School'.

- **Purpose:** To retrieve your essential energy from the
  past so that it is available to you in the present to
  help you to co-create the future.

Preparation

Prepare the space and get music together if you want
it. It is important that you don't get disturbed and
that you are not concerned about disturbing others.
Remember that the basic intention of the work is to
release yourself from the effect of difficult or traumatic
situations and to regain energy from any situation
where you lost it. The intention to heal, not to take
'energetic revenge' or dump energy, is important.
Sending any 'negative' energy back home and making
space to call back, move and embody original essence
or soul qualities are what make the process effective
and take it a step further than expressing yourself or
'discharging'.

Choose one specific event to work with from your past.
We recommend that you choose something simple to
begin with.

You can do this alone or choose to work with a friend
who can witness your journey and whose journey you
can witness too.

The Process

Create ritual space by lighting a candle, cleansing the space with sage or your favourite incense and calling the elemental powers, your ancestors, guardians, allies and any other help you can. Set up your mandala by standing in the middle of your space and, in your mind's eye, putting the different elements that you will be working with in their places. Call on the Tree of Life and feel your roots sinking down, your strong and fluid trunk in the centre and your branches reaching up. Remember the wise elder who lives in the centre of your heart. They know you well and are able to create the field of love in which healing can happen. Ask them to stand to the right of your mandala and visualize them there supporting and witnessing you. Behind you, get a feeling of the event you are going to work with. To your left, visualize the light of the soul essence or quality that may have been dimmed or lost as a result of this event. In front of you, envisage yourself as you will be as you grow and make more space for the soul within you. Visualize a big extractor fan above you to catch whatever energy is released through the process and send it 'home'. Imagine switching it on just as you begin the process.

Step to your right to stand next to your wise elder. Look over your mandala, taking note of whatever you sense is in the past, its effect in the present and the essence or soul quality that left in order to protect you and went to Soul School to learn all that you need to know and await the right moment to return to you.

Tell the story of what happened in the third person, as if it were about someone you once knew. Do not step into the event. Simply see it there as if you were watching a piece of theatre. The details are important, so include them if you know them. If you do not know the original event, describe whatever you sense of it and also the effect it is having on you in the present. Open yourself up to the new perspectives that can come about through engaging with this process.

Step back into the centre of your mandala, consciously ground yourself and start to move and consciously prepare your body by giving each part back to the dancer inside you. You need free and moving energy to do this work. Work with the element of earth to ground yourself. Allow yourself to feel the support of the Great Mother beneath you.

Once you are grounded and have brought your energy into circulation, allow yourself to feel in your body how the event feels for you now, in the present. Let yourself experience the impact the event still has on your body, your feeling and your thinking now, and keep moving. Yes, definitely keep moving!

Now call the fire, take courage and step back into the event. Let the fire be your ally and ask it to illuminate you, protect and support you to experience the integrity of your own circle, and give you strength. Allow yourself, without censorship, to give expression to whatever needs expression in movement, voice and word. Direct your energy towards a specific point, but not back at the person involved. Your intent is crucial here. You are not doing this for revenge. You are not doing this to dump energy. You are doing this for healing. It is important to allow yourself to move, communicate and express any energy that was either suppressed at the time or simply not safe or appropriate to demonstrate in the circumstances.

As the dancer, using the element of water as your ally, step inside the pattern, feeling or thought system that is connected to this event and do the work of disintegrating it by moving from the inside out. Consciously direct your thoughts, feeling and movement towards releasing the energy that has been blocking you or holding you back.

If the energy you are dancing to release will not move, respect this. It simply may not be time to release it. When stories have deep roots, you may first need to gain a little more energy by dealing with a few smaller stories on the same theme. Vibration and what is often called 'shaking medicine' are keys that can help you release the energy. Remember how the butterfly vibrates inside the cocoon when it is ready to be released. Visualize the energy rising into a spiral above you and being taken home. Ask the healing power of water to soften you and purify you as you dance.

This next part of the process is most effective when you are calm, focused and feeling grateful for what you have learned from this event or belief. You cannot force this, but you can invite it. Even if you are not aware of the teachings this situation has given you, it is good to say thank you to life for these teachings, if you can. Step back into the centre of your mandala and, turning to your left, call back the light that you may have dimmed as a result of this event into the space you have created. It is useful to say out loud: 'I call back the light of my own soul or freedom or truth that wasn't welcome in this situation.' It may be a specific quality or a specific 'soul piece'.

Now step into that place in your mandala and experience yourself directly as this essence. Find the movement, feeling, gifts and language for this returning or new part of the self. To what level are you ready to be integrated back into this dancer's life? Is there anything you need from the dancer in order to return?

When you have explored this, step back into the centre and receive whatever is ready to be integrated. Feel free to 'dialogue' with the returning part of your essential self and take time to feel the energy returning. We like to see this returning energy as light, and it is the dancer within you who 'physicalizes' this light in movement and thereby finds its dance. Let the wind be your ally here, uplifting you and giving you the perspective of new possibilities and open space. Feel the air all around you.

Get a sense of this returning energy becoming part of you again and welcome it in as you move freely. Turn towards the dreaming part of your mandala, the future you. See yourself acting in the world in a way that will help you to know for sure that you are free of any limiting effect this event has had on you and your life. Even more effective is to see yourself taking a specific action or being a specific way within the next seven days that 'bridges' this healing into the fabric of your day-to-day life. Step into this 'dream' and dance it as if it were happening now. Let yourself feel the feelings. Get right into it.

Once you've done this, turn back towards the centre and wink as if you were letting the dancer know that you had grounded this new dream. Step back into the centre and wink back. When you find yourself 'living this dream' within the next seven days, wink again at the dancer who did this SEER process. This is called 'bridging the dream' and it's also a lot of fun and a sweet moment of victory!

Back in the present, get a feeling for how this work has transformed your attitude towards this past event. It has now become part of your life experience and wisdom and, if it is not already, it will eventually support you in living more fully in the present.

Your last task is to find an incantation or a magical mantra, made up of movement, feeling and thought, that integrates the new state that your journey has created. Always phrase this in the present, for instance: 'At all times, I am connected to my medicine' or 'All that I need to give and create today and all the days of my life flows through me easily, effortlessly and gracefully.' The more you let yourself feel this statement is true now, the more powerful it will be. Dancing it, saying the words out loud and feeling it is a powerful way to plant this dream seed in your body, heart and mind. Remember that, as Tony Robbins says, 'Repetition is the mother of skill.'

Rest and allow all of this to sink into you, right into your bones, into your very cells! Feel the difference inside you. You have planted a seed which, with care and attention, will grow and become part of the garden of your soul. Take it in and breathe it out. Thank your witness and call them back into the centre of your heart. Give thanks and release your guardians and allies back to their freedom. Light some incense to cleanse the space again. Congratulations! Job done!

You now have a medicine bag of tools to help you be with your past, both on an ancestral level and on a personal level. Let's move to the next gateway, the central gateway in the Movement Medicine mandala, the present. See you there.

Chapter 15
The Fifth Gateway: The Present

'Yesterday's the past, tomorrow's the future, but today is a gift. That's why it's called the present.'

Bill Keane, cartoonist

Everything that happens happens in the present. Now, this moment, is the creative cauldron. It is the fulcrum between heaven and Earth, between past and future, between me and we, and between roots and branches. It is where all the polarities meet: receptive and active, feminine and masculine, being and doing, acceptance and intention.

To be present is both to witness and to participate fully in the dance of life. And to be aligned in body, heart and mind. It means to have the past behind you as a support and the future ahead of you as shiny and inviting as a freshly stretched canvas.

Those moments when we step out of rehashing the past and planning the future and into the miracle that is happening now are invariably gateways into the magical essence of life. They can happen any time, any place. The rattling sound of wheels on a marble floor, or the smell of freshly baked bread, or a tragedy, or a moment of falling in love can wipe out the tick-tock time machine, stop us in our tracks and deliver us into the grace of now. Now is holy and now is as ordinary as it gets. And now is the time and here is the place where creation happens. In ancient times, all roads were said to lead to Rome. In the Movement Medicine mandala, all roads lead to this moment, vibrating with the potential that is here and now.

The Power of Presence

The marriage of action with acceptance, laced with a grand dose of gratitude and happiness, is the deepest medicine we have found on our journey so far. What is this medicine for? It's for co-creating a life that is fulfilling now and a future that will make us and our descendants smile from spinning top to toe.

So in the present, right here and now, the invitation is always to receive all that is happening with acceptance, love and kindness. Accepting how something is is not the same as agreeing with or liking it. However, if you can relax in the acceptance of reality, as it is, without fighting it or judging it, you have a ground from which to grow. And once you have established a direction, through intent and sustained action, you can relax and follow the flow as your intention meets and interweaves with the energetic fluxes of everyday life. The relationship between your will and the will of the Great Spirit often results in something more majestic, surprising and magical than anything you could have ever dreamed up alone. This is the dance of co-creation in action.

This present moment is the result of the past – of what we individually and collectively thought, felt and did over a long timescale. And what we think, feel and do now is creating the future. The age-old 'secret' recently hijacked by the new age idiom 'You create your own reality' speaks of this truth, but in our opinion, the way this is often used reflects an inflated and incomplete view of our individual power. We prefer to say that we co-create with reality. We are not isolated islands. We are profoundly interconnected and deeply social beings. We live in a complex and interrelated world. We are constantly constructing our perception and the meaning we give to any situation. You can choose to make this process more conscious and thereby create more choice for yourself, but at the same time the context in which you do so has been created by what you have inherited from your personal and our collective past.

We live our lives in tides and forces much stronger and longer lasting than we are. Yet we are part of these tides and we affect them consciously and unconsciously, every day, every moment. So the subtle task of this central gateway is to wake up to our power and to our responsibility, without falling into illusions of grandeur. We are invited to humbly accept our relative insignificance, without imagining that who we are and what we do does not matter. Everything matters. Everything makes a difference.

So how do we cast off our preoccupation with the past and future and drink from the golden chalice of the present? As usual, the physical body is the anchor. It lives, breathes, moves and exists in the present. To be conscious in the body, and to allow the heart and the mind to be focused in the body, is to be present. And being present immediately confers the gift of presence.

Becoming Present

- *Intention:* To cultivate presence.

- *Purpose:* To connect what's inside with what's outside and what's outside with what's inside.

Create a space in which to work and get yourself present in body, heart and mind through your Movement Medicine practice or any other tool you have.

Become still and listen to your breathing. Feel your breath as it touches your throat and lungs. Rest in its rhythm and gently slow it down. Let yourself sit down into your bottom, letting your imaginary tail root down into the ground. Let the back of your neck lengthen, the crown of your head lift and your ribs widen, giving your heart breathing space.

Gently fill yourself with awareness, sweeping your attention through the whole body and including everything that is true now. Whatever emotional qualities you find, simply allow them to be. Give them breath and spacious, loving kindness. It's like gently blowing up a balloon, imagining all the cells breathing, until you are brimful with the soft shimmer of consciousness from your toes to your fingers. If you can't feel this, visualize it. If you can't visualize it, simply focus your mind on the invitation to inhabit this present moment in the body.

Imagine sunlight shining inside you and receive this light as the love of life. Expand your awareness to fill the orb of space immediately around you, offering it the same kind of spacious, loving kindness. Then expand further to a bigger sphere around you, this time including in your awareness the web of relationships you exist in, family, friends and colleagues. The quality of presence will probably feel different as the sphere of awareness gets bigger. Let it be as it is and go on offering spacious loving kindness to your relations. Then follow the connections out to the bigger web, which inevitably will eventually encompass the whole world and all the beings in it.

Sit for a while in this global sphere of awareness, breathing in and out with the spirit of life on Earth and offering spacious loving kindness and gratitude for life.

Then slowly bring your awareness back in until you rest in your own skin again. Focus on the feeling of being present in body, heart and mind and find a 'mantra of presence' to help you to ground the experience, something like: 'Here I am, my body is at home here and I am at home in my body. My heart is at home here and I am at home in my heart. My mind is at peace here and I am at peace in my mind.'

Where Are We Now?

We live in exciting times. Nature shows us in every season that change is part of the cycle of life. And we are in the midst of a massive change. The climate is changing much faster than predicted, the markets are straining under the pressure of what some say is the end of capitalism and all kinds of prophecies tell us that we're in for a difficult ride over the next few years.

More than ever, we need to be grounded in the essential truths that both keep us focused in the present and motivate us to act for the future.

As a human race, we have done some extraordinary things. We have developed our technology, our art, our medicine and our communication, and yet, since the Industrial Revolution, we have been moving gradually closer and closer to our own destruction. We have already lost swathes of species and destabilized the whole web of life on planet Earth. We have the power, but not yet, it seems, the wisdom to wield it with consciousness.

In the film challengingly called *The Age of Stupid*, the massive importance of the decisions we need to take collectively over the next few years is poignantly brought to our attention. Set in 2050, the film features Pete Postlethwaite speaking to us and wondering why, with all the information we had at our disposal, we pressed ahead with our way of living in the name of the free market (and what a misnomer that has turned out to be!), even as our own destruction became more and more inevitable.

As a species we are a bit like a youth who has been given a powerful tool without getting any instruction on how to use it and what it is for. The way we have used our technological power to make war and used the Earth to fuel our consumerist passions has led us to the brink. Here we are in a global crisis that invites us to take an evolutionary quantum leap of consciousness to find the wisdom to accompany our power. And this means developing a way of thinking, feeling and acting that includes individuality, the collective and the Earth as a whole. Life on Earth, at least for us, now depends on finding ways to live that are sustainable for us all. Without doubt, we have the creativity to do so. The question is: 'Do we have the will?' Or 'How bad do things have to get before we find that will?'

The good news is that a systemic, ecological and global way of thinking, feeling and acting is breaking through in many fields. It does not preclude individual freedom, conscience, creativity or expression. Indeed, each of us finding and embodying our unique truth is an essential part of the whole dance of human awakening.

Whilst working with shamans in the Amazon rainforest in Peru, we experienced the enormous power of the primal energy that is the living Earth. For many years, we had worried that our collective actions might destroy her. However, when we saw her magnificent force, we understood that though we might do a lot to unbalance her, it is ultimately we humans who will pay the price for our arrogance.

> **Ya'Acov:** *I have just returned from spending two weeks in the Colombian mountains with a group of fellow travellers. We were with Kajuyali, a Colombian shaman, and six beautiful human beings from the Kogi people, including two Mamas (the Kogi name for shamans). The Kogis, who became well known through a BBC documentary made about them in the nineties by Alan Ereira, have now come down from their mountain home to give us a message. They tell us that we have stopped experiencing this planet as a living being and ourselves as her guardians. Mother Nature herself has reached tipping point in her ability to sustain herself as we plunder her depths for resources. Like so many other tribal peoples who still retain a connection to the Earth as a living and conscious being, the Kogi have realized that if we are to survive, they need to speak out on her behalf.*
>
> *The gathering was also attended by shamans from the Lakota tradition of North America and other local shamans and healers. Through the many ceremonies they shared with us, we were given opportunity after opportunity to*

experience directly our symbiotic relationship with the health of the planet we live on.

The indigenous peoples of the Earth bring us an important message, but it is time to realize that each and every individual and each and every culture on the planet has a piece of the puzzle. I grew up being told that my people, the Jewish people, were the chosen people. I always rejected that idea as dangerous. All peoples are chosen for something and we will only find peace if we learn to respect our own culture and to listen to and learn from the wisdom of other systems and cultures too.

Many prophecies speak of the coming together of the eagle and the condor. I take that to mean that now is the time for us to share the very best of all the different approaches to being a human being on this planet. We need to find the humility to learn from one another and the confidence to share what we have discovered. One way or another, the Great Choreographer, Nature and all manifestations of the divine are trying to communicate with us. We are being warned from all sides and at the same time we are being invited to remember the very thing that will give us the happiness that so many of us long for: we are one family and that family includes all the kingdoms of this Earth.

Basics

Food, shelter, human kindness and love are our basic needs, yet they are not afforded to millions upon millions of the world's population. Statistics tell us that there are 27 million slaves in the world today, many of them children, and that is not counting those other millions, many of them also children, whose pay is basically a slave's wage. So it could be fairly asked, 'Isn't it a luxury to think about *being present* and dancing? Aren't there more important things to take care of?'

Of course there are and yet we look around and see that despite the massive advances in technology that in the West have given us a longer life expectancy and in many ways have made life easier, as a culture we seem to be deeply dissatisfied, alienated and unhappy. We have lost the balance between the material and the spiritual. We have forgotten the importance of knowing who we are, what truly matters to us and what we are connected to. And for us, and maybe for you too, movement has been the medicine that has helped us to shatter the spell that has separated body and spirit and generated the systems of fear, selfishness, greed and destruction that have led us to where we are.

The predominant culture in these times is driven by the belief that the Earth is a resource for us to use. It is driven by the need for constant growth. It offers a constant stream of things designed to fill the hole inside us, caused by the loss of a simple connection to the ground under our feet. This loss of roots is an advertiser's dream and a living planet's nightmare. Our friend Roland told us that he'd heard something fascinating on the radio. Over 5,100 years ago there was the dawning of what some call the Age of Kali. Many Vedic texts mention the general ill effects of this age, but one in particular, the *Bhagavat Purana*, is quite specific:

> *'People will suffer shortages of natural resources, yet be overburdened with taxes. They will no longer look after their elderly parents. The cities will be dominated by thieves. But justice will be bought through power and influence. Businesses will run on deceit; and wealth alone will determine a person's status. It will be considered unholy to be poor. But, even in ordinary circumstances, people will*

accept degraded livelihoods. Men and women will unite on the basis of superficial attraction and each will be judged by their expertise in sex. Beauty will depend on one's hairstyle. People will confuse audacity with truth; hypocrisy becomes a virtue; and someone good at juggling words will be considered a great scholar. Political leaders will cling to power and greedily squabble over territory. They will go to war with no real cause. Their efforts to exploit the bounty of the land and sea will make the Earth lament.'

Sound familiar?

Without our roots, we are easy prey. Just as the tree without strong roots may well lose its life in the storm, human beings who have lost a sense of their own ground find that their lives and dreams are shaped for them by a multitude of external forces. Whilst acknowledging its necessary subjectivity, it is important to recognize the reality of where we are as a world. And to acknowledge that change happens in the present and begins inside each of us. We each have a part to play and a responsibility to play it as well as we can according to our own truth. Our future will be created by the actions we take in the present. As our friend Jake Chapman often reminds us, most change has been brought about by passionate and determined individuals.

Dissatisfaction

Dissatisfaction makes us good shoppers. Fear of not keeping up, fear of that empty feeling inside keeps us addicted to consumption and keeps us separated from our own instincts.

In 1929 Charles F. Kettering, the Director of General Motors Research Laboratories, wrote an article entitled: 'Keeping the Consumer Dissatisfied'. In it, he argued that satisfied consumers just wouldn't want to buy the next product that came online and that that wasn't good for business. A little later on, Edward Bernays, the nephew of Sigmund Freud, was the first person to take his uncle's ideas and utilize them to manipulate the masses. He showed American corporations how they could make people want things they didn't need by systematically linking mass-produced goods to their unconscious desires. Advertising techniques have become more subtle and sophisticated over the years and we have been hypnotized *en masse* to equate happiness with the latest gadget or product to come off the mass-production line. And yet, research shows that beyond basic standards of survival, there is no correlation between happiness and owning more and more things. And because the majority are trapped in what the Achuar people of Ecuador call 'the dream of the north', it seems sane to continue even as we sleepwalk towards our own destruction.

Radical Happiness

'*I slept and dreamt that life was joy. I awoke and saw that life was service. I acted and behold, service was joy.*'

Rabindranath Tagore

So how do we start? Get present, get moving, get happy and take action! Genuine happiness, based on who you are and the love and gratitude you feel right now, is the most radical antidote to our collective hypnosis. There is happiness already there inside you awaiting your attention and your permission to take centre stage in your life. And gratitude is, both in our experience and according to many recent scientific studies, the golden key to happiness. As an intentional practice, it can transform our lives. For that to happen, though, we need the ground of acceptance and action, so that's where we're headed next.

Acceptance

The word 'integrity' comes from the Latin *integr-* or *integer*, meaning 'whole' and 'entire'. To have the sort of integrity which comes from wholeness requires a deep honesty. It means being willing to look your demons *and* angels in the eye. Befriending them and then becoming their conductor rather than their victim is a journey that requires compassion, tenderness, courage and tough love. The reward is the freedom to relax inside yourself, in complete acceptance, knowing that there is nothing to hide.

To become conscious of ourselves and, with honesty and kindness, acknowledge our own condition, we need to cultivate the inner friend or witness, the part of ourselves that can reflect lovingly and truthfully on ourselves and our lives. Cultivating access to the witness is a core practice in many traditions. The witness has a natural quietness and calm and consequently has access to the silent wisdom that we so often drown out with the noise of our busy minds.

For instance, imagine a situation at work. A colleague or boss says something that makes you feel small or undervalued. If you have a history of this kind of interaction, your mind will pull up all similar circumstances from the past, thus intensifying the feelings of humiliation, and before you know it, you are drowning in a confusing whirlwind of emotions. In the meantime, the witness in you is watching the situation. They are watching all the feelings arising with dispassionate calm. They are watching the meanings and the stories arising, and they are breathing, staying aware of the body and staying grounded and present. If you're willing to listen, they may ask you: 'Is it possible that the meaning you are giving to the words you heard is not the whole truth?' If you can hear this, you can step out of the story and into the open possibility that is the present moment.

Developing the Witness

- *Intention:* To cultivate the ability to witness what is happening now with kindness and compassion.

- *Purpose:* To be able to live in a way that is more rooted in the present moment.

Familiarize yourself with the instructions to this recipe first, so that you can do it without interrupting yourself.

Create a space in which to work and get yourself present in body, heart and mind through your Movement Medicine practice or any other tool you have. Then lie down and make yourself warm and comfortable.

When you are feeling connected and centred, let your breathing become natural and listen to your body relaxing and sinking into the ground.

Then see yourself climbing a mountain. See, hear, smell and feel your journey. Feel your feet on the path. You realize you are on a quest to seek out the wisdom of the witness who has an overview of your life and who lives in the present moment. You know that this witness has been with you all of your life.

After a while, up above you, you see a cave. At the mouth of the cave stands a figure, watching you. As you come closer, you see their face. It's like looking in a

mirror. The reflection is calm, still, loving and peaceful.
You sense the witness's benevolence and wisdom. As
you come even closer, they open their arms and greet
you and invite you to sit down with them at a fire at
the mouth of the cave. This witness is like the external
twin of the wise elder in your heart. As you meet the
witness, you feel the connection through your heart.

As you sit down, you see the view for the first time. It
sweeps down the mountain and across the plains. You
realize that you are overlooking the landscape of your
life. Important people, places and situations from your
life, are laid out, as if in miniature, far below.

The witness speaks. They have some things to tell you,
or ask you. You, too, have some things to tell and to
ask. You speak together and take stock of your life
together. You feel bathed in the understanding, love
and compassion in which the witness is holding you.

After some time, you realize that it will soon be time
to go. The witness asks if you have one last request or
question. If you do, then ask it. Take time to receive
the response. When this is done, you feel in your pocket
and find that you have the perfect gift or offering for
this wise part of the self who is the witness of your
life. As you give it, they slip into your hands a gift of
their own. You receive it, even if you don't understand
its significance now. You bow deeply to each other,
then you make your way back down the mountain. The
witness remains at the mouth of the cave for a while,
smiling down at you. When you next look up, they have
gone and the cave has disappeared.

Returning to the base of the mountain, you lie down
in a comfortable glade, close your eyes and take in all

that has happened. When you are ready, you stretch and wake up to find that the glade has transformed into your sacred space.

Take some moments to write down the conversation with your witness. You may even find that more detail comes through as you write. If you were given new information or a new direction for your life, and if you know it is right for you, act on it.

You can revisit the witness any time you need to and as you get to know them you will find that you have instant access to their view, which is always a view from the present.

Intention and Action

We've focused on presence, on being and becoming a witness to the present. Presence is half the story in this gateway. The other thing that can only happen in the present is action. And if we are to change our individual and collective dreams, we need presence to give birth to action.

Susannah: *As a child, I attended a little village primary school called Girton Glebe. In the last year we had a teacher called Miss Brown. Looking back, I guess she was a bit of a hippy. Anyway, she taught us all the guitar and I learned a few basic chords and would drive my parents insane singing the beautiful and melancholy 'Land of the Silver Birch' over and over again. Much later, in my thirties, as I slowly developed my musical know-how, I felt the urge to reconnect with the guitar. So I asked Ya'Acov for one as a birthday present. It sat there for years, its steel strings biting my tender fingers so hard each time I tried to play it that I gave up. Eventually I swapped it for a nylon-string* *guitar, but then that sat there instead. Eventually, we both decided to learn the guitar. But still it sat there. Then Ya'Acov bought a guitar, we got a teacher and now we're playing, and faster than I could have dreamed, I'm making a good noise!*

The other day I was driving to a workshop I was going to teach, listening to some amazing Schubert. The violins sang through my heart and I felt so grateful for my music teacher, Julian Marshall. After a few surges of this feeling I decided to call him. Leaving a message on his answerphone, I was flooded with love and gratitude, and this stayed with me for the whole workshop. It was good for him too! I was struck again by the difference between feeling something, and turning it into action.

I can spend so much time feeling the weight of everything I have to do. When I simply do it, it's often so much simpler than I imagined.

As you may have heard from the ancient Chinese philosopher Lao Tzu, 'The longest journey begins with a single step.'

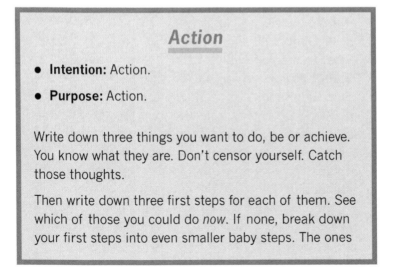

Action

- **Intention:** Action.
- **Purpose:** Action.

Write down three things you want to do, be or achieve. You know what they are. Don't censor yourself. Catch those thoughts.

Then write down three first steps for each of them. See which of those you could do *now*. If none, break down your first steps into even smaller baby steps. The ones you can do now, *do now!* Then catch the wave you have created and go on riding it.

Sometimes this process can move so fast it can be disorientating. If so, keep feeling the ground, breathing and taking the time to reorientate yourself in the new reality you are creating. Sometimes it takes great persistence, patience and faith. Create some micro-practices for yourself, things you can do in 30 seconds which change your mood and set you back up for good living. Make that phone call, clean that fridge, stop and take a breath, roll your shoulders and sing that song!

The 21 Gratitudes

Ya'Acov: *I was recently teaching an ancestor workshop in Ireland. Ireland is always a special place for me to visit. As well as being beautiful and magical, it's where my great grandparents arrived as refugees from the Ukraine at the end of the nineteenth century. They didn't speak any English and they had been told that the boat they were on was taking them to America. The story goes that it took them six weeks to realize that they weren't in the USA at all but in Ireland. My grandfather, one of their nine children, used to tell me wonderful stories of his childhood in Dublin, and the bakery where he would go to get the morning bread is still there.*

During the workshop, we spent a lot of time acknowledging the lives of our ancestors. We danced their grief and their joys, their suffering and their loves, with the explicit intention of finding more compassion for and connection to them. It was a deep and powerful weekend of work.

On the Sunday morning, I awoke from a dream in which I was told the following: 'Ya'Acov, it's good and beautiful and right to acknowledge and honour the past. It is good to honour our ancestors and make a place for them in our lives. And there is a question that is even more important for you and all your brothers and sisters.' I waited for the punchline. It arrived with simplicity and force: 'What kind of ancestor will you be?'

Wow! What a question! It is our actions right now, today, that will determine our future.

Several years ago, I had a dream in which I was told to practise a meditation called 'The 21 Gratitudes'. The dream teachers explained that it was good practice for the heart to begin and end the day with a few thank yous. And so I started the practice, regardless of what kind of day I'd had or how I felt when I woke up in the morning. It's been one of the most powerful and transformational choices I've made. After I'd experienced the effect on my life, we started to make the meditation part of our Movement Medicine work.

Since many of us have become accustomed to focus on what is missing in our lives, it is quite a change of mind and heart to focus on what *is* working. And, as we already know, a change of mind and heart will certainly create a change in our physical state too. The 21 Gratitudes have been part of our daily practice for many years now and the effects have touched every area of our lives. To begin and end each day with gratitude means that we begin and end each day with a sense of warmth, connection and increasing happiness as we acknowledge again and again the bounty and creative challenges of our lives. From being part of the culture of complaint, we have relocated to the land of satisfaction. And far from making us complacent, it is this radical sense of 'OK-ness' that gives us the energy and the will to do our work and to be part of the groundswell of evolution, consciousness and change that is sweeping the planet.

The 21 Gratitudes

- **Intention:** To feel gratitude and cultivate a ground of true happiness.

- **Purpose:** To refocus your mind on the goodness in your life.

The thing we love about this recipe is that it can be done anywhere and at any time. Our favourite time and place for it is in the woods walking our dog. It's good to be able to move and to speak out loud and to embody the feelings of gratitude as they arise, but simply closing your eyes and focusing is fine too, as is sharing this with a friend.

There are many times when we wake up in the morning when we don't feel like doing this meditation, and on those days, as we suggest for you too, it's better to do 'The 42 Gratitudes'! The thing is, there are always genuine things to say thank you for. And the act of focusing on and feeling them is very empowering. It changes our perception and expands our point of view, and this is turn helps us to see and relate to the world in a different way.

We suggest you do this practice daily for the next nine months. We're quite sure that you'll notice a difference quickly, but it takes nine months for a child to be born so we suggest you give yourself the time to give birth to the new state of mind that the 21 Gratitudes bring.

So how does it work? The key is simply to begin and to keep going. Start with yourself ('I give thanks for my heart for beating more than 100,000 times every day and keeping me alive, I give thanks for my eyes that see, ears that hear, etc') and move on to the people you love. Start with those closest to you and keep moving out in ever-expanding circles to include all those whom you are in contact with. Gratitude in all forms of relationship is the key to bringing out the best in people. Move on to giving thanks for the Earth, the sun, the rain, the air, your home and all the things in your environment that support your life. Many indigenous cultures hold the view that our gratitude for the living Earth beneath us is the minimum payment that we need to offer daily to stay in balance. Try it and see. From there, move on to thank your ancestors and all the guides and guardians you have in the spirit world. Maybe you are aware of them and maybe not. Say thank you anyway. At the very least, our ancestors' existence has given us the opportunity to live now and they deserve to be remembered and thanked. Finally, find your way of giving thanks to the Creator.

It's important with this meditation to say thank you to the Great Choreographer for the challenges you are facing in your life as well as the easy times. Remember that part of the intention behind this recipe is to change your attitude from distrust and dissatisfaction to trust and contentment with all that life is providing for you. As we have already said, we have chosen to work with the meaning that life is intelligent and provides each one of us with perfectly choreographed situations in which we can learn and grow. And we are likely to learn as much from difficulty as we are from ease.

Don't get hung up on counting the gratitudes. Just make sure to do at least 21. If you're anything like us, your thank yous will become more and more poetic and heartfelt and you simply will not be able to stop. Maybe we'll meet one day on a train or at a bus stop and we'll just look over at each other and say, 'Ah, you too ... thank you!'

Once you've got the hang of it, you can integrate this recipe with your Movement Medicine practice and include the 21 Gratitudes in the dance as you continue to integrate the life of the dance into the dance of your life.

As we move on to the sixth gateway, this meditation of gratitude will form the ground of the work we will do together to co-create a future that is a blessing for all our relations.

Chapter 16
The Sixth Gateway:
The Future

'I have become my own version of an optimist. If I can't make it through one door, I'll go through another door – or I'll make a door. Something terrific will come, no matter how dark the present.'

Rabindranath Tagore

We are living in times of change. Prophecies of doom abound as old certainties crumble as fast as the Arctic ice. Whether it's the end of the Mayan Long Count calendar, scheduled for 21 December 2012, or the glut of apocalyptic sci-fi movies, there are a huge number of fearful images being pumped into the airwaves about the future. Perhaps it doesn't sell newspapers or books or cinema seats, but can you remember the last time someone offered you a beautiful vision of future possibility?

Who Creates?

So how does the future get created? Is it destiny? Is it fate? Do we create it ourselves? Our own experience has led us to sense that reality is a multi-layered matrix that is much deeper and more intricate than a human brain can hold. It's a mystery, and we like it like that. The force of evolution has a long time frame that was in motion way before the first human had their first thought. But we are part of it. We all have a big part to play in the creation of the future through the ways we think, feel and act.

We are only just beginning to understand the power of focused thought in a focused body-heart-mind. In Lynne McTaggart's book *The Intention Experiment*, she tells us how it is possible to measure the effect of focused thought on house plants, even when we are at a distance from them. Think of watering your favourite plant and gently cleaning its leaves and it will respond. Think about burning one of its leaves and the graph that is measuring its energy field will jump off the page in apparent panic.

When we add feeling, communication and action to our thoughts, we end up with a potent instrument of change. In recent times, books selling old secrets about how to attract wealth and happiness have ended up on the bestseller lists. The Universal Law of Attraction, made popular through the movie *The Secret*, tells us that what you manifest in your life is the result of your thoughts, both conscious and unconscious. In apparent resonance with this, many indigenous cultures that still live close to the Earth tell us that what we experience in the physical world is the result of what we 'dream' in the world of spirit.

In 1987 we went to a camp to celebrate something called the Harmonic Convergence. We sat with 300 other people in a huge circle and were told by the camp organizers that we were responsible for 'keeping the energy clean'. We weren't quite sure what they meant until one of our good friends, who was suffering from a debilitating illness and was feeling a little depressed, was told to go a nearby field and deal with her 'negative karma' and stop 'polluting' the camp with her bad vibes. We were horrified. A group of us got together to try to find a creative response to this 'positivity Fascism'. So, at three in the morning, dressed in rags and covered in mud, we danced and howled around the camp, in and out of tipis and tents, embodying the collective shadow of the camp and, in our own way, attempting to bring a little balance and humour to the situation.

We tell this story because it encapsulates the dangers of using a little ancient wisdom to shore up a belief system that thrives on blame and separation in the name of so-called consciousness. The difference between the new age view that 'you create your own reality' and the indigenous view that 'we are dreaming this world into being' is contained in the use of the words 'we' and 'you'. We have often heard people talking about someone's illness or misfortune and suggesting that the person involved is responsible for creating it through some kind of repressed emotion or negative thought pattern. This 'blame the victim' way of understanding is a simplification of the complex web of causality. We are not islands. We are linked through time and space in a complex web of multi-factorial relationships. Yes, there is great wisdom in self-responsibility, yet at the same time we need to balance this with an awareness of how interlinked we are. Stuart Davis, the 'punk monk', wrote this in his critique of the film *The Secret* and the philosophies behind it:

'I have an ego, and it has desires, and it's healthy and appropriate for that level of my being to seek fulfilment. My thoughts are powerful, and my feelings matter. But the Universe does not reconfigure reality to accommodate the personal preferences of my ego every time an impulse comes through my reptilian brain stem. That is not just narcissism, it's KOSMIC narcissism, and that is what The Secret *is selling.'*

In the sixth gateway, it is extremely important to get clear about the differences between the needs of the small self and the Soul Self who is already dreaming in interconnection with all of creation.

Our first medicine teacher, a lovely warm bear of a man called Batty Thunder Bear, put it beautifully. He told us about the difference between 'the personal dream', which involves taking care of our own needs, and the 'sacred dream,' which involves knowing who we are and what we are here to contribute. He talked about the task of bringing the personal dream into alignment with the sacred dream.

The personal dream needs to be in balance in order for the sacred dream to be sustainable in our lives. Gabrielle Roth gave us a useful question to ask ourselves: 'What do we need on a material and physical level in order to be able to give the best of ourselves?'

We have learned that life becomes a joy when the personal dream serves the sacred dream and when the sacred dream is in alignment with the dream of the Great Spirit.

We believe that each of has a sacred dream that is calling us. We believe that each of us has something to contribute to the whole. The quest to discover your sacred dream and then live it is a contemporary lifelong vision quest.

Following the Golden Thread

To have a vision for your life is to have a light to follow in times of darkness. It gives you a purpose. Without a vision or a purpose, we are like feathers in the wind, blown from pillar to post.

But the thing with visions, as already noted, is that they rarely come with instruction manuals. Many people think that seeing a vision in spirit means it will instantly manifest in the physical realm. And if that doesn't happen, they feel they have failed, or they lose faith in the vision itself. But it's up to us to do the work.

For instance, imagine you have a vision of creating a beautiful garden at home. You see it in great detail – the waterfall, the variety of plant and animal life, juicy vegetables growing and maybe a fireplace to sit around and tell stories. You awaken from your vision on a cold November day and look out into your back garden. What you see is a mess. It's overgrown. You realize that you have a choice: either you dismiss your vision as some otherworldly dream or you take a deep breath, go outside, pick up your spade and start digging.

All visions, big and small, work in the same way. It takes courage to dream them and then courage to do the work. Yet to find a vision worthy of you and then to work to realize it is perhaps the most fulfilling journey you can take. And a good vision will keep on evolving with you. If you pay attention, it will leave you clues on the road or in the sky, and we call following those little signs 'following the golden thread'.

When a vision comes, to follow it means to set out on an adventurous path. Thinking metaphorically, it is good to remember that if you set out to climb to the top of a mountain, for much of the time you will probably not be able to see the summit. When the destination is out of sight, it takes faith to keep placing one foot in front of the other. And things of worth often take time, and sometimes our job is simply to keep dancing and keep the flame alight.

We don't know where this quote is from, but we love it:

> *'You have become fully human when you start to plant trees under which you know full well you will never sit yourself.'*

Golden Thread Stories

Susannah: *I was lying in my student room in Leeds wondering what to do with my life. I was 19 and had just left medical school after three weeks. Lying there on that quiet dark night, scared and jubilant, I knew I had just taken my life into my own hands. I knew that leaving medical school was right. It had felt impossible, but I had done it, and the sky hadn't fallen on my head. The dean had been very respectful and given me the chance to come back the following year if I wanted.*

Lying there in the dark, I asked myself what I really, really wanted to do with my life. Immediately I saw a huge amphitheatre full of people and on the stage there was a woman gagged and tied to a chair. In the theatre piece she freed herself, reclaiming her body, her movement, her voice and her freedom to become a singing, dancing powerhouse of heart art. I knew this was a symbol of a 'way'. I knew this way involved music, dance, drums, singing, bodywork and theatre. It was about healing, but what was it and how could I move towards it? I knew that theatre or dance school wouldn't lead me there. Nor would any university course I could imagine. I knew I would have to find my way one step at a time.

I asked myself what I had really, really wanted to do when I was little. That was very clear: my first ambition had been to be a caveman(!) and my second to be a hunter-gatherer. I had a vague idea that there was a university course called anthropology which was something to do with hunter-gatherers. Of course, I wanted to be a tribal person, not to learn about them, but as I was still in the paradigm of going to university, it made sense.

I knew that if I was ever going to find the theatre of my vision, London would be a good place to be. So the following year I began to study anthropology at UCL. I learned a lot on that degree course for which I am grateful, though not very much about how to be a hunter-gatherer. I did learn some useful generic things about healing ritual and, most of all, took a good look at the prism of our own culture and the language through which we perceive 'other cultures' and life in general. And I learned that though I love the conceptual world of ideas, I'm not interested in words separated from experience. I walked out at the end of it, vowing I would never again use my life to learn about what some people thought about what other people thought about what some other people actually did.

During my degree I discovered Gestalt psychotherapy and began to train as a therapist at the Gestalt Centre in London. What a relief to be received as a feeling, expressive person! And I danced, discovering West African dance with Orchestra Jazzira in Balls Pond Road, and Whirligig, which was then in Leicester Square. One weekend I went on a movement course and came back to college unable to sit still, wiggling through the library, humming over my books.

In May 1986, whilst revising for my finals, I met Ya'Acov in the garden of my women's squat in Stoke Newington. By the autumn we were a couple and soon we discovered the Deer Tribe and began to study the Sweet Medicine Sun Dance path. This was another sort of medicine!

In 1988, at a women's workshop at Hazlewood House in Devon, Heather Moon Owl led us on a ceremony called the 'death doll, life doll' ceremony. It involved making a 'doll' to represent everything we were ready to let go of in our lives. Mine was more of a 'thing' than a doll, but anyway, it was made. I sang and danced and said what I was letting go of into it and then buried it.

We had a sweat lodge and sweated, prayed and purified. In the morning, with Heather's instruction, we began to make our 'life dolls' to represent the sacred dream we wanted to call into our lives. We were instructed to do this with no thought, just let our hands get on with it. It took all day. I had no idea what I was making or what it represented, but it slowly came into being, a long curvy snake of wood decorated with ribbons and flowers. As dusk fell, Heather blessed the amazing and very individual creations. One by one, we held our objects and gave voice to the dream they held.

My turn came late at night. As I took my object in my hands, I felt electrified, jolted into life. I had no idea what would come out of my mouth. When the words came, they surprised me, but they were strong and sure. It was all about dance – dance as a healing path, for myself and as my offering. As if from above, I saw a snake of people of all ages and all races of the world dancing and singing together through the rainforest. It was a beautiful and potent image which continues to guide me now.

I was surprised. I had always loved to dance, but I had never thought of it as my central path. But this vision was very clear. It resonated with the theatre vision from six years before, too. I was happy, because there was no question about it. There was a deep, still certainty in me. But again I had no idea where to go to learn about it.

A few weeks later, at home with Ya'Acov in London, I received an Open Gate brochure which someone had sent me (no idea who, but thank you!) In it was the syllabus for Gabrielle Roth's first teacher training. I was astonished. This was it. Totally. Gabrielle's words resonated all the way through me. I was thunderstruck. Then I got the price tag. Whoops! Oh dear, maybe later on when I've got some money! So I put the information away, only to get it out again a few weeks later for another look. Then I saw that there was a weekend course with Gabrielle for £100. I could just about afford that, so off I went, and so did Ya'Acov, who had quite independently decided to book onto the same workshop.

When Gabrielle started to speak, I started to cry. These were the words I'd been longing to hear. They were the words I would have said myself if I had known how to find them. They watered a desert inside me I hadn't even known was there. And the dance! What bliss to be guided through so many aspects of allowing and letting go in connection with others. Gabrielle and her work held the door open for me to walk through into the rest of my life.

After 18 years, as we followed our own golden thread, our work eventually diverged from the 5 Rhythms. And in the Peruvian Amazon, suddenly there we were, singing and dancing in the rainforest.

Singing and music are now becoming a central part of my path, along with the dance. The forest and trees are important both metaphorically and literally. My original vision has yet to be fully manifested, but I see clearly that I am still being guided by what was revealed in that vision and that I am on my way there.

Ya'Acov: *Just before I met Gabrielle, I had spent the whole summer doing workshops with Arwyn Dreamwalker, a mixed-blood medicine woman who embodied a quite enchanting blend of Cherokee and Irish roots. At that time, Arwyn had a working partner called Bridget. They* *were a great team. I was working my way from workshop to workshop, just going home to earn enough as a photographer to get myself to the next venue. I was 23 and a shamanic experience junkie. I leaped from ceremony to ceremony, trying to recover the innocent connection I had had with spirit as a child.*

During one ceremony, I had what remains to this day one of the most terrifying moments of my life. Looking into a mirror with Susannah at one shoulder and a giant of a man called Blue Thunder Horse at the other, I saw myself as a child dying in one of the gas chambers of Auschwitz. Suddenly, I wasn't watching the movie, I was in it. I started to scream and completely lost control as I tried to put out the candle lighting the room. Once I had been calmed down and returned to the present, Arwyn suggested that I should go to Auschwitz and dance for the souls of the child I had become and the many thousands of children who had died in that way. I promised to do so.

It took me 13 years to feel strong enough to fulfil my pledge. I went with a group of German psychotherapists. I remember the cold terror of my dreams on the train to Auschwitz. We spent the day taking the guided tour around the museum. We visited Birkenau and eventually returned to our hotel, weary and emotionally drained. I hadn't been able to dance there during the day, as it had felt inappropriate, so I told the group that I was going back at night to dance and pray as I had promised to do all those years before.

Two of the women decided to come with me and we walked through the icy streets of the town and back out towards the infamous landmark of the watchtower of Auschwitz-Birkenau. It was dark and the gates were locked, but I managed to persuade the Polish guard to let us in so that we could pray. During the daytime, there had been an eerie peace about the place, but at night it was a different story. To me, it felt crowded with the unquiet suffering of the men, women and children who had died there.

We started our ceremony at the end of the railway track where prisoners were offloaded and either sent to work or straight to the gas chambers. I could see the Nazi doctor who had made the life-and-death decisions and I started to move and pray in Hebrew. I felt a flood of strength and at the same time I was close to collapsing. But I danced my defiance and I sang my Jewish song.

We moved from there to one of the women's barracks. Inside, I could hear voices and once again I nearly lost consciousness. I prayed in Hebrew again and my German friends repeated the words after me. Without warning, I felt my face and body contorting and I felt the terror of an old Russian woman who was desperately trying to hide a baby who had been born in the barracks. I don't speak Russian, but for a few moments I was back in that time and whispering fluently about how we needed to keep this child alive. I got out of there as quickly as I could and danced some of the veils of untold stories.

Finally, it was time to go to the gas chambers. I was in an altered state that wasn't much fun. It was a cold and cloudy night, but when we arrived at the ruins of the chambers, the clouds parted for a moment and the light of the moon illuminated what looked to me like a large group of shivering children. I danced my prayers and my grief and told the children that we were leaving. They followed me along the train track, Pied-Piper style, towards the locked gates.

As we came closer, the guard who had let us in appeared. He looked to me like the ferryman who takes the souls of the dead over the River Styx. I reached into my pocket for all the money I had, marched up to him and said: 'This money is for the souls of these children. Do you accept it?'

I'm sure he didn't understand me, but he took the money and unlocked the gates. As we went through, the moon slipped through the clouds and a shaft of silver-gold light touched the ground just beyond us. I told the children to jump into the light and watched as each one of them found their way home.

I was elated and exhausted. I thought that my pledge had been fulfilled and that my story with Auschwitz had come to an end. But the golden thread was just about to take another twist.

That night, I had a dream in which I was at a festival called the Phoenix Festival. It was happening in the town of Auschwitz and it was 'a celebration of every human being's ability to transform the ashes of their suffering into hope, possibility and new life through the power of creativity and forgiveness'. I saw Germans and Palestinians and Israelis and people from many areas of conflict around the world engaged in a process of profound listening and healing. I saw musicians and artists and spiritual leaders from all the world's traditions engaged in ceremonies and celebrations of diversity and unity. And I knew that the festival was happening every two years at different places in the world that had witnessed great suffering. I found an official and asked him who had organized the event. He laughed at me and said: 'You did.' And then I woke up.

Following the golden thread, I started to teach in Israel and Palestine (I had already been teaching in Germany for some years) and to take the first steps towards this dream becoming a reality. Once I started my work in the Middle East, I realized that it might not happen in my lifetime, but it has already inspired some deep healing and I will continue to take the steps, one at a time, to bring it about.

Your
Vision

There are many ways of finding your vision. Some of us seem to be born knowing what we are here for, others trip over it in the street. Some find it in maturity or even old age, whilst others struggle with a lack of purpose for many years. There is a grace and mystery in the timing for each of us. And yet we would not recommend passively waiting. 'Ask and you shall receive' is not a casual dictum.

When vision is passionately and patiently sought and we are willing to tolerate the discomfort of not knowing for as long as it takes, we open the way to finding out what we are here for. In the meantime, there is lots to be done discovering and developing our potential and enjoying what we are, what we do and life itself.

In recent times, ancient ceremonies from many different world traditions have been brought back into our consciousness by travelling shamans who have sensed the spiritual poverty in the western world. In our own journeys, we have been blessed to work with many great healers and teachers. For several years, we were honoured to carry peace pipes through our connection with Native American traditions. We learned about the sweat lodge ceremony, participated in a sun dance and took part in different vision quest ceremonies.

Throughout all of these ceremonies, as previously mentioned, we felt as if we were being loaned sacred tools to help us to remember what we had individually and collectively forgotten. Over the years, as our connection to the land, the elements and our own ancestors grew, we slowly received our own medicine. It took shape on the dance floors of Europe and the USA and in the wildness and primal beauty of the Arctic and the Amazon forest. And our journey has been guided every step of the way by the visions we received at different times. Now we find it necessary to create spaces regularly throughout the year to make sure that we are staying on track. Sometimes visions change, and when they do, it's necessary to change with them.

The bottom line is that it is vital for us all to make some kind of time and space to put ourselves in the wider context of the wilderness (or as close to it as we can get) and to sit down, shut up and just listen for a while. Most people in our busy western world are so busy chasing after somebody else's imported dream that they don't get to hear the quiet voice of their own spirit. Imagine arriving in the last hours of your life and never having asked yourself: 'What is truly important to me in this life? What do I love? What matters? Who am I? What am I for?' This is the purpose of the vision quest. It's a time to listen to the deeper truths that guide your life and to honour your ancestors and ask them for their support. And if you do have a guiding vision or dream already illuminating the way for you, it's a time to strengthen your connections, update your vision if necessary and witness and give thanks for the journey so far.

A Mini Vision Quest

- **Intention:** To find or strengthen your connection to the highest purpose in your life.

- **Purpose:** To take full responsibility for what you are here for and to find the resources to bring your dreams to Earth for the benefit of family, community and all your relations. And for you too, because it's a joy and a challenge to be with the magnificent mirror that is nature herself.

You are invited to spend a day alone in a beautiful place in nature. You need somewhere where you won't be disturbed. As always with this kind of ceremony, it is important to be properly prepared and to make sure that some people know where you will be and what time you are expecting to return. Make sure to take advice from someone with local knowledge if you're going somewhere unfamiliar to you.

Take an emergency kit, also water and a water purifier if necessary so that you can refill when you need to. Take a journal as well and something to sit on. It is customary to fast for the day, taking in water only, but only do this if you feel strong enough and if necessary, take medical advice.

Begin your journey before sunrise so that you can be walking to your destination as the sun rises. Pay attention to the world around you and to the thoughts that arise as you walk to your chosen place. Try to drop your expectations of how the day will be.

Once you arrive at your chosen spot, speak to the spirit of the place, telling it who you are and what you are doing there and ask for permission to be there.

You might like to use some of the different movement meditations from earlier in the book to help you to ground yourself, focus and align body, heart and mind. Creating the sense of standing at the centre of your own circle and calling in your allies, support, ancestors and anything else helpful is a fine idea.

Here is a list of questions to help you on your vision quest. They are meant as a guide, but this is not a religion, so be sure to trust your own instincts during the day.

Section 1: Your Power
These questions will help you to review the different aspects of your being that are connected to your power as the co-creator of your life:

1. What is your relationship to your yin energy, your ability to receive life and rest in the ground of your own being? And, in the spirit of accepting what is so and becoming all you can be, how would you like it to be?

2. What is your relationship to your yang energy, your ability to act with clear intent in the interests of your own and others' evolution? And, in the spirit of accepting what is so and becoming all you can be, how would you like it to be?

3. What is your relationship to your own sexual/creative energy? And, in the spirit of accepting what is so and becoming all you can be, how would you like it to be?

4. How is your ability to manifest your dreams in accordance with your highest purpose? How close is your life to how you dream it can be? And, in the spirit of accepting what is so and becoming all you can be, how would you like it to be?

5. What is your relationship to the divine and your spiritual journey and practice? And, in the spirit of accepting what is so and becoming all you can be, how would you like it to be?

Section 2: Your Life
The second section will help you to get an overview of your life and open yourself up to asking for a vision:

1. What have been the most challenging times of your life and what have you learned from them?

2. What have been the best times of your life and what have you learned from them?

3. If you were to die tomorrow, would you feel fulfilled and at peace? If not, what would you need to do to change that?

4. What does your soul dream? What are you here for? Pray for a vision.

Make sure to spend some time sitting quietly, listening to the sounds around you and enjoying the place you are in.

When you receive a vision (and this can come through thoughts, images, a feeling or a signal from the world around you), give thanks. It is a good idea to share the vision with your ancestors by imagining those who love you around you and asking them for their feedback. It is also a good idea to imagine your descendants around you and share your vision with them so that you can see what you have received in the context of the past, the present and the future. If you don't receive a vision during the time of your quest, it is important to realize that the vision quest is as much about holding the question as deeply and sincerely as you can. Patience is often necessary. Remember that answers can drop in at any time.

As you are asking the questions, be conscious of the mirror that nature is. A willow is a willow; it is not trying to be an oak. The river is the river; it is not trying to be an eagle. In nature, everything is itself and if you pay attention, it will reflect back the answers to your questions, sometimes in ways that are easy to understand and sometimes in ways that are more poetic and enigmatic.

Feel free to dance, to walk, to sing and, most importantly, to listen.

Once you have finished, find a way of thanking the spirit of the place and making an offering. From the first section of questions, we suggest you create incantations based on the intention to bring into being the best relationship you can with your creative energy (*see below*). It is also a good idea to share the story of your day with a supportive friend. It can even be good to do this ceremony in tandem with a friend so that you can support each other before and afterwards. Enjoy!

This recipe is meant as an introduction to the very deep and ancient practice of vision quests. If you try this and would like to go further, we recommend you seek guidance from one of the many organizations that offer vision quests with excellent support throughout, including the School of Movement Medicine.

Incantations

Hopefully you will have found some interesting answers to the questions we suggested you focus on. The answers to the questions in Section 1 form the basis of a daily practice we suggest to all our students. It goes hand in hand with the 21 Gratitudes and it is best done in movement.

At the beginning of this chapter, we wrote about the creative power we have when we focus and align the body (movement), the heart (passion) and the mind (dreams and ideas). As you will have gathered by now, we strongly suggest that when you are focusing on what you want to create in your life, you make a distinction between your personal and sacred dream. It is important to know what you need on the material level in order to give the best of yourself in all areas of your life. We need to make conscious choices. Do you wish to give your life energy to creating as much material wealth as you can for yourself, regardless of the consequences. Perhaps you wish to dedicate your life energy to co-creating a life that is as much in harmony as it can be with the realization that all life is interconnected? We are given free will. Ultimately, it is up to each one of us to find the truth in our own hearts and decide whether or not to live in alignment with that truth. This is why the journey through these three gateways is called the Journey of Responsibility. We believe that it is time that we woke up to our responsibilities to each other and to our role as guardians of the future. As a species we have arrived at the point in our journey where we need to expand our hearts beyond the separate self to a place of practical compassion and connection – connection with our ancestors, our family, our communities, the animals, nature, the spirit world, the whole shebang.

So, as we move on to the last recipe in this gateway, we invite you to make the choices that will honour the past and your ancestors, the present and your own needs, and the future and those who will inherit the results of our actions today.

Embodied Incantations

- **Intention:** To focus your creative power on co-creating a future that honours your deepest purpose as a human being.
- **Purpose:** To play your part fully in co-creating our future together.

An incantation is a magical calling. It is an active way of harnessing the creative power that each of us has for the benefit of all. Incantations develop and change over time. The more you work with them, the more specific they become. You craft them through practice and they develop with you. An incantation works best when you fully engage the creative resources of your body, heart and mind.

Take your answers from Section 1 of the vision quest questions and distil each one down into a simple sentence. It is important that it is written as if it were already fully manifest in the present. For example, 'I would like to be able to receive the gifts of my life fully and enjoy my physical body in a sensual way,' becomes: 'I fully receive the gifts of my life and my body is a delightful and sensual home for my spirit.'

When creating incantations, remember that you don't have to begin with the perfectly crafted piece. It will develop as you work with it. And it is always good to create them within the context of working for the highest benefit of all.

We suggest that you add the incantations to your regular Movement Medicine practice. It is a good idea to take the elemental journey and work with your incantations in movement. What you are looking for is the feeling that what you are focusing on is already fully present and embodied. You sense what it feels like to have achieved this goal and be resting in this state of being. This is called 'stepping into the dream'.

Create a space in which to work and get yourself present in body, heart and mind through your Movement Medicine practice or any other tool you have. Call all your allies and support. Say your incantations out loud and let yourself be passionate. It is the power of your heart, in alignment with the spoken word and the moving body, that gives momentum to your incantations. In the end, each incantation has a dance, a feeling and the power of the spoken word. It is good to repeat the incantation several times. Get into the emotion, the joy of co-creating with life for the highest benefit of all. You are taking your place in the circle of people around the world who are daring to dream a beautiful future.

Incantations do not work by themselves. They are the equivalent of preparing the ground and planting seeds in it. But once you've planted the seeds, you need to take care of them. And that means two things: 1) you need to take the actions that will help them to grow in a sustained way; and 2) you need acceptance of and, if possible, gratitude for where you are right now. Now is all there is, so why not enjoy the journey?

Living with Chaos

We can be pretty sure that the world in which you are reading this book will be different from the world in which we are writing it. Change is gathering pace. Hopefully, by the time you are reading, renewable energy on micro and macro scales will have transformed the oil economy. And people everywhere, from individuals to governments and corporations, will have realized that we are one world and that our wellbeing and that of our children cannot be separated from that of all other life on Earth.

The likelihood is that whichever way we are headed there will be a certain amount of chaos to navigate our way through as the ways in which we have lived cease to be viable. Chaos has a destructive as well as a creative edge and the waves of change that we will be surfing will demand poise, balance, love and courage from each one of us.

We recently heard about some research done with people who had survived a variety of disasters. The researchers looked for common factors and this is what they found:

- Survivors trusted the evidence of their own senses and instincts over what they were told by those in 'authority'.

- Survivors were more likely to be cautious types, as highly skilled adventurous types often took risks which led to their deaths.

- Survivors had a strong bond of love with someone whom they were determined to return to or stay with and they did not give up on their quest.

As the basis for a little advice pack for chaotic times, this research isn't bad. So trust your instincts and your sense of what is happening and what you need to do. Don't be macho. Let love inspire and strengthen you. And never give up!

Our future is in the balance. We strongly believe that we have the intelligence, the capability and the heart to turn this ship around. Each individual has a piece of the puzzle. We ourselves have seen thousands of people over the years take the healing journey from rigidity to fluidity, from self-doubt to self-confidence and from separate and scared to connected and trusting. We know this is possible. And we know that we each have the power to play our part.

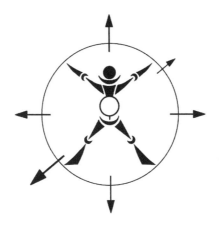

...• Part IV •...

Living the Dream

Chapter 17
Introduction to Living the Dream

'The dream was always running ahead of me. To catch up, to live for a moment in unison with it, that was the miracle.'

Anaïs Nin

Freshly returned from a dynamic, inspiring and hopeful vision for the future, it's time to go forward together.

If you have taken the journey with us up to this point, you will have discovered strengths and weaknesses along the way. You will have discovered that some parts of you are more developed and mature than others. You will have aligned body, heart and mind a little more through the Journey of Empowerment. And through the Journey of Responsibility, your relationship with your past will be in a process of metamorphosis. From a place of presence and knowing your personal dream and your sacred dream, you will have tools to support you in the ongoing and joyful task of co-creating the future.

Living the Dream is the place where all the work of the previous six gateways can start to bear seriously juicy fruit. It's time to both bring in the harvest and share it out.

As we progress on our journeys, it becomes more and more important to pay attention to the basics. So we want to remind you of the importance of the dancing dialogue between acceptance and growth. You are perfect as you are *and* you are a work in progress. We all are.

When we stand with our favourite trees in the woods behind our house and as we watch them change through the seasons, we have to bow time and time again to their wisdom. They are the perfect teachers of this dance. When it's time for them to rest, they rest. When it's time for them to grow, they grow. When it's time for them to flower and to offer their fruit, they do just that. For them, every dance is loyal to its season. We keep mentioning this because we see, in ourselves and in our friends, students and teachers, just how easy it is to think we should be somewhere other than where we are. And from there, it's a short hop into the nasty habit of beating ourselves with the rod of self-criticism. On the other hand, some of us get attached to an idea that since everything is perfect as it is, why should we do anything? Our tree friends answer that question every spring when a new cycle of creativity literally bursts through their buds. We grow because it's time. We let go because it's time. We rest because it's time. To everything, its season. And so it is with us humans too.

So as we begin this final trilogy, we want to bow before the Great Mystery of timing. Whatever season you are in and whatever your current circumstances, the work of these three gateways is dependent on this mystery.

The seventh gateway is *Fulfilment*. We hear the word 'fulfilment' as *being filled full*. In other words, to be full of life, to be deeply satisfied and to be on the journey to fully manifesting the unique human being we are.

We cannot fake or force fulfilment. Finding our way there is both a choice about how we perceive the present and a lifelong journey of discovery. It involves us as individuals and as members of the community of life on Earth. Though fulfilment is a very personal thing, we will share with you some of the keys that we have discovered that we hope will help you along your way.

The eighth gateway is *Interconnection*. Acknowledgement of the interconnectedness of life dissolves the illusion of separateness. Though any man, woman or nation may try to be an island, the challenges we face today may ultimately wake us up to the reality that we are one interdependent family of life here on Earth. At this point in human evolution we have an opportunity to marry this pragmatic, everyday awareness of our interconnection with the more enigmatic energetic realm. Science and mysticism have never been closer. Many current scientific discoveries are leading to an understanding of the universe that is similar to the mystical awakenings that have inspired poets, artists and seekers for millennia.

The many traditions of ecstatic dance, from the ancient to the modern, have always offered a route to the direct experience of this unified state. What an opportunity we have today to find an inclusive paradigm which is 'both/and' rather than 'either/or'. We can learn from both conceptual and experiential understandings of life. We can celebrate both the unique expression of each individual *and* the power and potential of our deeper unity or interconnectedness.

The ninth gateway is *Realization*. To write about realization is to attempt to describe the indescribable. But to those fortunate enough to have a moment of pure enlightenment, this lightning flash of direct experience gives a context to their existence that puts everything else into perspective.

The importance of these experiences is in what people choose to do with them. Jack Kornfield's excellent book entitled

After the Ecstasy, the Laundry gives a clue. According to him, experiences of realization are more common than we may think. The fact is that the person who has had the highest of experiences still has to live in this world with all its suffering and challenges and yes, they still need to do their laundry. The challenge we face is to live in this world with all of its harshness, cruelty, beauty and mystery, acknowledging our own humanity as well as our divinity and, with a strong heart, making our contribution as best as we can.

Living the Dream is what you are already doing, consciously or not. The combined work of the 9 Gateways gives us the option to make our dreaming and our actions more conscious. It gives the possibility of working with the raw materials we are given and creating with life in our own way.

Your true being is your own offering. Born out of your own searching and your own experiences, it is your gift to this world. Whether that means living in a hut in the forest or singing your song on stage, that offering is yours to give and it is your ticket to living the dream.

And what a paradox living the dream is. On the one hand, we are dreaming our world into being as consciously as we can. And on the other, we are constantly asked to let go and consent more deeply to the unknown mysterious unfolding of life.

Chapter 18
The Seventh Gateway: Fulfilment

'There is something within me, what is it then? How can I make myself useful and what end can I serve? I cannot tell you how happy I am to have taken up drawing again. I have been thinking of it, but I have always considered the thing impossible and beyond my reach.'

Vincent Van Gogh, aged 27, writing to his brother Theo

'Fulfilment: Satisfaction or happiness as a result of fully developing one's abilities or character.'

New Oxford American Dictionary

Fulfilment requires acceptance and enjoyment of life as it comes and of who you are. At the same time, it is the ongoing process of becoming who you can be, fulfilling your own sense of purpose and through this making a contribution to the world which is meaningful to you. And lastly, at least for most of us, it is intimately associated with love and connection with others.

Fulfilment is not a fixed state of being. It comes and goes. Or it might be more accurate to say that it is always there and that it is we who come and go. We cannot force fulfilment to enter the house of our lives, but we can prepare the rooms and open the door.

As we have been writing this chapter, we've been asking ourselves and others: 'What is fulfilment?' One of the consistent answers we've got is that fulfilment is related to deep engagement and commitment. Whatever we are doing, no matter how apparently mundane, if we are deeply engaged it will become fulfilling. Watering the garden can be deeply fulfilling or it can be a mundane chore. So can playing a concert, building a house or helping two people communicate better.

Choosing this Life

Many years ago we were sitting together in meditation and we both independently saw the spirit of our child and said 'yes' to him. Susannah heard his spirit. Ya'Acov saw his light. We both felt certain that Susannah was pregnant and though each of us felt deeply happy about it, we were sure that the other one would be freaked out. It took us 24 hours to find the courage to tell each other. When we did eventually get round to it, we both fell into a deeply blissful and peaceful place and were certain that Susannah was pregnant. As it turned out, she wasn't, but this experience led us to say 'yes' a month later. Later, in sharing this story with some friends, they told us about a tradition in which it is said that 28 days before conception there is a meeting in heaven between the parents and child and their respective angels. During that meeting, a contract is made in which all parties agree to provide each other with the experiences that will help the soul to grow.

Like many things in this realm, whether that is ultimately true or not seems less important to us than how such a belief can be used. We've seen many people use it in very empowering ways. One student who had had a truly awful childhood told us that at one point in her healing, she found it very strengthening to come to an understanding that she had chosen these situations. It helped her to step out of feeling like a victim and into choosing to truly make the most out of her experiences. She considered her childhood to have been the perfect training ground for the amazing work she ended up doing with children who had suffered abuse like her. She is certainly one of the people who comes most strongly to mind for us when we think of fulfilment. So it is in that spirit that we offer you this meditation.

I Chose this Life

- **Intention:** To experiment with the empowering story that you chose your life.

- **Purpose:** To empower your sense of purpose and to step firmly onto the road of fulfilment.

Take a notebook and pen, create a space in which to work and get yourself present in body, heart and mind through your Movement Medicine practice or any other tool you have.

When you have moved for a while and feel focused, sit quietly or feel free to go on moving. Some people find it easier to 'take journeys' when they are still and have their eyes closed. Others prefer to move and keep their eyes open.

Visualize the Tree of Life in front of you and travel up the trunk to the level of the branches and leaves. You are in the upper world. There is a beautiful space there that you feel called to. It could be a tipi or a palace or a wide open plain, depending on your preference. You are there to witness an event.

As you sit there waiting, some bright beings arrive. You recognize them as the spirits of your parents and yourself before you were born. Each one is accompanied by an angel or a guide. You watch as they sit down and begin to talk. They are discussing your purpose in life and you listen intently. They talk about some of the challenges that you will face and what they are designed to teach you. They talk about what it will take for you to both feel fulfilled and to fulfil your purpose.

When they are finished, they all turn to you and smile. You thank them and say anything you want to say to them and when you have finished, you leave in different directions.

You return to the Tree and go back to your own sacred space. Make sure that you ground yourself and then write down all that you saw and heard. It's great to do this with a friend or friends and to support each other to celebrate what is working in your lives. There is a recipe later in the chapter that will help you to do just that.

Naturally, there are 'easy-flow' kind of days and 'edgy-stressy' kind of days in the great classroom of life. Sometimes we stumble along for many years, following the scent of a dream or a desire. Sometimes we take a dead-end road and end up in the middle of nowhere. But in our experience, when we look back, there has always been some little gem of a lesson we picked up in 'Nowhere Town'.

The windings and turnings of our own journeys have given us a tad more wisdom. When once we used to panic or fret about having lost the way, these days we have a little more of a sense of humour about the whole 'manifesting your vision' dance. Life is the Great Choreographer and often has other plans for us. There is in fact a mysterious and dynamic dance going on between the Great Choreographer and our own dreams and creative will. And, as we have mentioned before, things work best for us if our own will dances with that of the Great Spirit. That leads to true fulfillment.

The Movement Medicine BASIC Plan for Fulfilment

We have found that following a dream and working to bring it into reality are about as fulfilling as it gets. When you are making your contribution, there is a deep sense of fulfilment that radiates out from you and inspires others around you to do the same.

There are a few keys we've learned along the way that have helped us to evolve and make our contribution in a balanced and sustainable way. So here's our five-point BASIC Plan for a

Fun and Fascinating Journey on the Road of Fulfilment. Have a good trip, and see you somewhere on the road!

1. The **B**liss Key

2. Take **A**ction

3. **S**avour the Journey

4. Stay **I**nspired

5. Get and Stay **C**onnected.

1. The Bliss Key

So, realizing our purpose will bring fulfilment, but how do we know what that purpose is? Some people seem to be born knowing or discover it early on in their lives. Others need time, patience and a certain determination to find out what it is. We've already looked at this, and the vision quest recipe on pages 204–208 will support you in bringing your purpose into focus. If you haven't made the time to go and do it yet, stop reading about it. Put this book down, pack your bag, get out there into nature and, as it is said: 'Go and cry for a vision.'

When we were in our twenties we read Joseph Campbell's brilliant piece of career advice: 'Follow your bliss.' What an exciting way to see life. What we are here to be, to do and to become is exactly what engages us, fascinates us and yes, plants us regularly and firmly in a state of bliss.

As you grew up and went through your 'education', were you encouraged to find out what switched you on so totally that you forgot yourself and time disappeared and you became pure involvement? If so, you are one of the lucky few. If not, no problem. It's never – and we mean *never* – too late. This state is what athletes call being 'in the zone'. And it can arise in any activity in which we allow ourselves to be completely immersed and engaged.

Susannah: *I love sailing. I love horse riding. I love dancing and singing. I love working with groups. One essential quality that all these share is that in them I am working with a powerful force which I can guide if I listen deeply and communicate clearly, respecting the nature of the beast I am dancing with. In each, I have to be strong and sensitive, receptive and active, and if I and we get it right, we can travel far and thrillingly and have wonderful adventures together.*

What is my Bliss?

- **Intention:** To check in with why you are here.
- **Purpose:** To connect with your purpose as a compass for life.

Create a space in which to work and get yourself present in body, heart and mind through your Movement Medicine practice or any other tool you have. Then lie down, make yourself comfortable and ask yourself whichever of these questions interests you. Don't censor your answers at all – just let your imagination roam free in the land of possibility.

- 'What turns me on?'
- 'When have I experienced the bliss of total involvement? What makes me buzz?'
- 'What is really, really important to me in this life?'
- 'What did I love as a child?'
- 'What did I dream of being or doing as a child?'
- 'If I was an old man or woman, facing my death, what would make me feel really happy and proud and content with my life?'

> - And the ultimate request: 'Please give me at least a glimpse of what my life would look like if I was truly living in alignment with my purpose, using my gifts and guided by my bliss.'
>
> Write down, or draw, the answers without any attachment to them being 'right' and without any fear of them being 'wrong.' Just get them down on paper so you can see them. Then let the questions and your answers marinate in you as you go about your life. Sometimes the important answers come when we are just dropping off to sleep, or waking up, or opening or closing a door, or often whilst dancing. Hold the questions deeply and your own answers will come. Listen.
>
> There are no right or wrong answers to these questions. The answers are intimate matters of the soul.

2. Take Action

Once you have a sense of your purpose, of what you want to create, experience and contribute, there comes a pivotal moment. Look at your life as it is. Look at where you put your energy, what you *do* with the precious minutes and hours and days. Look at your purpose. Is the life you are living now aligned with it? Is the way you are being and behaving moving you towards the fulfilment of it? If not, why not indulge in a few howls of anguish, stamp your feet and then accept the humanity of your predicament?

We talked about action in the chapter on the present and it's sufficiently important for us to mention it again here. It's time to ask yourself whether you are ready to take action to become the designer of your life. Are you up for fulfilment? Are you willing to change?

Once you know what you want – what you really, really want – action is the key. Remember, sustained, committed action over time is the difference between those dreams which vanish in a puff of smoke and those which come to life. It includes communication, sharing and often finding others with whom to work and play towards manifesting your dreams.

It's very important to honour the small steps. They are far more potent than you may believe. What is life but the result of zillions of tiny decisions and actions which stack up to create what is? When it comes to fulfilment, we need to be strong, to have faith and courage, and most importantly, to persist. As Walt Disney said (and he should know!): 'All our dreams can come true if we have the courage to pursue them.'

If you've decided that you are up for fulfilment and are willing to take action, you are ready for this meditation.

From Vision to Action

- **Intention:** To access our wisdom about what we need to do.

- **Purpose:** To find the actions which will keep us on the path of fulfilment.

Create a space in which to work and get yourself present in body, heart and mind through your Movement Medicine practice or any other tool you have. You can do this recipe by yourself, though it would be great to invite a friend over and to support each other with it.

Close your eyes and go into the 'realized dream', your vision of what your life would look like if you were truly living in alignment with your deep purpose, gifts and bliss. Imagine that it is real now. Feel it, breathe it, smell it, see it, hear it. You may want to move with it, sing with it, speak with it or write in it. If you write, write in the present tense, as if it's all happening now.

You may well find that this experience expands well beyond what you thought you knew. Again, don't worry about what is 'possible'. Find a quiet place at the centre of your visionary landscape and settle there, breathing in this place, this state and this way of being.

If you are doing this with a friend, ask each other: 'How did you get here?' Imagine there was a time when this was just a dream and ask each other to tell the story of how you got here. If you are alone, imagine a friend arrives in your dream reality and asks you to tell your story. Get out your notebook and write the story of how you got here, including what you did all those moons ago, after you had that vision in your sacred space, back in the year...

When you have finished, close your book. Take a moment to return to this vision landscape. Feel, breathe, smell, taste, see and hear it all. Take it all in, with your friend by your side. When you are ready, thank the vision, thank your friend, thank yourself and say goodbye for now, knowing that you can come back here at any time, and let yourself transport back into your sacred space.

Ground yourself, give yourself a rub, stretch, drink a glass of water slowly and give yourself some time to take in what you discovered.

In a few hours, or the next day, return to your work space and read the story in your book. Let it be an

> inspiration for action. Decide on a step that you could take *now*. What do you need to do this month to keep your momentum moving? How will your life look in three years' time?
>
> The key here is to keep on taking definite and practical steps that will create the momentum you need. And by the way, don't forget to enjoy the journey!

Susannah got this imaging technique from an inspirational man she worked with many years ago called Warren Ziegler. Warren devoted his life to developing techniques of envisioning and future creation which supported people in their quest to get in touch with their spirit and their potential.

Susannah: *It was with Warren that I learned how to jump into the 'realized dream' and then figure out how I had got there. For me, those short and intense days with Warren laid a foundation of understanding the power of image and imagination, which has now found its way to you in this book. Warren died in 2004, but his work continues. His books and tapes are a great reservoir of guidance about, as he called it, 'en-spiriting' our lives.*

Once you start to take action, be patient. Sometimes things start to change quickly, like a stack of dominoes that has just been waiting for the initial shift. But often things take time. Life took a long while to get where it is now. It has momentum. To change track, you need to stay steady at the helm of your boat.

And timing is a great mystery. We do the work, we put in the hours, the commitment and the practice, and then one day, suddenly, we can play that tune, ride that bike, sing that song in public. We cannot control the timing of things. We must play our part and then surrender to the mysterious grace of it all.

And on the way, there will inevitably be days full of the detailed, everyday and sometimes mundane work that supports the unfurling of the big picture. We know you've heard it a million times that the art of creation is 10 per cent inspiration and 90 per cent perspiration. The trick is to learn to enjoy the sweat!

Susannah: *To enable our work, there is a backdrop of administration, deskwork and phone calls which takes up a large chunk of our time. Finding inspirational ways to work with this has been, and remains, a challenge for me. Remembering what it is all for is one key. Remembering that each detail matters and is part of the whole we are creating is another. Remembering that this too is a dance and that I can feel and enjoy my body even as I sit typing or filing is another. Most important of all is allowing each communication to be a chance to give and receive love and share a laugh and a moment of life with another human being. That really helps. You know how it is – we remember, we forget and we remember again.*

3. Savour the Journey

If fulfilment becomes something to aim for in the future, we are missing the point, the boat and the golden opportunity, which is only ever *now*. Fulfilment does not only depend on getting 'there' – it also comes from being fully engaged in the process of life. For most of us mortals, fulfilment is not a fixed state. It is, like the rest of life, in flux.

The key is to savour the journey, combining the acceptance and enjoyment of what is with the desire and drive for what could be. Each one of us has a different blend of these two energies. Some people are fulfilled by simply being. Others need a lot more doing and achieving. There is no right or wrong. Each style contributes something different to the world and each has its own challenges and delights. It's a matter of accepting and working with your nature, so that you can enjoy the journey as much as you can. Relish the process. Accept the challenges, difficulties, disappointments and successes. Savour the journey, the moment-to-moment being alive in it all.

And remember that sometimes your dreams, however deeply held and devotedly followed, don't come to pass. Or not in the way you had hoped for. But this does not mean that the intentions were wrong or that the work that went into them is wasted.

Susannah: *Ever since I was a little girl my wish, when cutting a cake or pulling on a wishbone from a roast chicken, has been for peace for the world. I have walked and demonstrated and been arrested and prayed and sung and danced for peace. And though peace is always present behind the chaos of our world, peace on the global scale and in the manifest form that I dream of is not here. The suffering in the world continues. Man's inhumanity to man continues and I have been part of conflicts myself which I did not know how to resolve. But the ardent longing and wishing and working for peace which the young and the mature me share is not wasted or belittled by its failure to succeed. We are either strengthened or weakened by life's realities and to a large degree that is our choice.*

Savouring the journey entails dealing with life's realities. They may not be all you would wish for, and at such times be gentle with yourself. Let your psyche retreat as well as advance. Stretch *and* relax. There are times when it is right for the warrior in us to charge forward with full focus and passion and there are times when we need to let our visions go, put our feet up, breathe in, watch the sun set and thoroughly nourish our being.

Ya'Acov: *I had a student a while ago who was, like myself, very driven. There is a big difference between being driven by a feeling of not being OK and being driven by the essence and passion of what we are here to give. Once, after a deep session of dance, my student told me that he felt inadequate amongst such a very fine circle of 'dancing warriors'. He started to give me all the reasons why he wasn't OK as he was. Feelings of inadequacy can be an inspiration to be the best we can be. But in this case, he was being harsh and his words had a ferocity and unkindness to them that could only have come from something he had taken on from the outside. I asked him where he thought this unkindness was coming from. He told me that his father had always given him a very hard time whenever he wasn't immediately perfect at whatever it was he was learning. I understood.*

I asked him what he did for a living now and he told me that he was a gardener. I asked him if he was a good gardener. He said that he had always been employed and that yes, he was a very good gardener.

'Do you shout at your plants and tell them how to grow?' I asked.

'Of course not!' he replied.

He got the point. We need a balance of kindness and strength in order to grow. The bluebells need the love of the fertile soil underneath them, the call of the sunlight and the blessing of the rain to invite them to share their beauty. In our own true natures, are we any different from the nature around us?

Full of Life

- **Intention**: To feel the sheer joy of being in a body.
- **Purpose:** To savour being who you are right now.

Go to your work space. Let your whole body move, stretch, breathe...

Now go through your entire body, moving gently, inviting yourself to experience pleasure in and through each part. Let your breath be like oil, lubricating, softening and opening your body to the flow of the pure and simple pleasure of being here, being in a body, feeling the texture of life.

If there are parts of your body which feel achy or sore, see if you can gently and consciously allow the achiness to help you feel more into the texture in the muscles, the joints. Invite pleasure to come in too, maybe mingling with the other sensations. You may be surprised at how powerful this can be and how much sensual pleasure we can invite into the body through simple attention, breath and sensitive movement.

Once you have gone through your whole body, imagine that you can feel the micro-vibration of all the billions of cells in your body buzzing with life. Allow yourself to feel full of life, literally full-filled.

Full to the brim, let your attention overflow into the space around you. Relish the colours and shapes of the space you are in. Go into your day taking pleasure in the texture of life, inner and outer. Notice the beauty of life around you, the small miracles that are happening all the time.

4. Stay Inspired

As on any other road, there are many pitfalls along the road of fulfilment. As we keep on saying, balance is the key. Excessive seriousness makes the outlook heavy. Too much work and not enough play and we all know what happened to Jack. We've just got back from watching *Dean Spanley* at our local cinema, which is housed in a beautiful old barn. There's a wonderful line in the film which is very relevant here. It's spoken by the character after whom the film is named. He's a rather eccentric dean in the local church. On being questioned about his belief in the possibility of reincarnation, he remarks: 'Certainty is the outcome of a closed mind.' In these days where fundamentalist views are vying for centre stage all around us, the dean's curiosity is a breath of fresh air.

When we're working towards a vision, and perhaps even more so when we're in the midst of manifesting one, it's vitally important to stay inspired, and to stay inspired means to stay open. A friend of ours who is a clown was speaking to an elder who had been clowning for more than 40 years and who was still full of zest and vitality. He asked him what kept him so alive in his work. The old clown quickly replied: 'Every day, try something new. The moment you stop taking risks, you die.'

In this gateway, we're concerned with being and becoming all you can be and giving all that you've got. So to stay fresh in this realm means many things. It means refreshing your own source of inspiration, which in turn means putting yourself in situations where you are learning new things. It means finding situations where your strengths are strengthened and your weaknesses are illuminated. And it means being willing to be very honest with yourself. We are creatures of habit and some habits simply don't serve us very well. Anything that keeps us from becoming dogmatic and keeps our bodies, hearts and minds open is a good thing.

A few years back we decided that it was important that each year we did something as complete beginners. So far, our pledge has led us to the wilds of the Amazon forest, an equally wild catamaran sailing course on the Menai Straits, the delights of salsa and learning the guitar. All of these things have contributed enormously to the development of our vision and to our fulfilment. We have also remained students within our field of work and have been blessed to meet a stream of amazing teachers. We suggest you ask yourself: 'What do I need to remain inspired?' We suggest you focus on physical, emotional and mental inspiration and think about the small things you can do on a regular basis to keep yourself balanced. After all, if you have a car, it needs maintenance from time to time. So do you. Enjoy!

5. Get and Stay Connected

In order to live this dream, we all need a community of support both within us and around us. Within us, that means kindness and acceptance when we fall short of our goals or when we're having a bad day. And it means connecting on a regular basis with that inner place of silent knowledge. Five minutes of silence, or breathing or moving or simply being, before the busyness of the day is worth its weight in gold. When people tell us that they don't have time to practise or to remember the guiding light that is directing their existence, we just say: 'No problem, get up five minutes earlier.' Each of us has to discover what we need and stay current as it changes, with the season, with the moon and with whatever is happening in our lives, but the important thing is to give yourself the time to connect.

As well as connecting to your own self and purpose, belonging to a network or community of good friends is a massive blessing. To have friends who are not afraid to love, challenge and be mirrors for us is so important. And to be able to laugh and, quite often, laugh at ourselves is a must. Think of the best times you've had with good friends. Do you get that warm smile deep down in the belly that tells you that fulfilment is a real and lived experience? If not, it may be time to dream such a circle of friends for yourself. A good place to start would be to ask yourself the question: 'How can I cultivate a sense of friendship with others as well as with myself?'

We all need guidance sometimes. Whether that comes from friends, family, mentors, teachers, a pack of tarot cards or a special place in nature, it's all good. Sometimes, especially when we begin a project or when we have an epiphany that we're trying to integrate into our lives, it may feel as though we're swimming against the tide as we get things going. But as we gather momentum, suddenly it is all much easier. And if we have friends who are heading in the same direction, it can feel effortless. So it's time to invite your friends to a party!

A Fulfilment Party

- **Intention:** To find out what fulfilment means to you and your friends.

- **Purpose:** To support each other in living a fulfilling life.

Invite your best friends over for a 'Fulfilment Party'. Explain to them that you are interested in what living a fulfilling life means to all of you and you'd like to try a fun experiment that will get you all helping each other.

Why not start with a delicious potluck meal by asking all your friends to bring over a favourite dish? Or why not have a little dance before you get down to the evening's main event?

Once you've loosened up, draw everyone together and ask them to write down the answers to a few questions.

Give them 15 minutes to answer them. The questions are:

1. Who are the most fulfilled people you have met?

2. What qualities make you think of them as being fulfilled?

3. What would living a fulfilled life mean to you?

Once you've all answered the questions, sit down together and share your answers. If you are more than six people there, it may be best to split into smaller groups so that you don't get overwhelmed by too much listening. Let the discussion unfold for as long as it needs to.

Once everyone has shared their answers, get them to answer another set of questions:

1. If you knew it was possible, what would you dare to dream for yourself and for the community of life on Earth?

2. What could you contribute to this dream?

3. What do you need to make more space for in your life and what do you need to cut back on in order to be more fulfilled?

4. Could you take the first step before you leave this party?

Discuss these answers, too, and before you end, get everyone to say out loud what their first step is. If you want to, agree to meet again to check in with how you're all getting on with Project Fulfilment. Use the BASIC map (*page 224*) to help you along the way. Before you know it, you'll have a new level of love, friendship and support in your life.

The bliss key, taking action, savouring the journey, staying inspired and getting and staying connected will support you in making the contribution that only you were designed to make in the world, and that is the surest way to enjoy your dance along the fulfilment road.

Through this last recipe, we have already stepped onto the bridge that will take us into the beautiful landscape that is the eighth gateway of the Movement Medicine mandala. From connection, it's just one short turn of the page to interconnection. See you there.

Chapter 19
The Eighth Gateway:
Interconnection

*'A human being is part of the whole called by us universe,
a part limited in time and space. We experience ourselves,
our thoughts and feelings as something separate from
the rest. A kind of optical delusion of consciousness. This
delusion is a kind of prison for us, restricting us to our
personal desires and to affection for a few persons nearest
to us. Our task must be to free ourselves from the prison
by widening our circle of compassion to embrace all living
creatures and the whole of nature in its beauty ... We shall
require a substantially new manner of thinking if mankind
is to survive.'*

Albert Einstein

We are not isolated. We are interconnected, physically and
energetically, in a complex whole that binds us together as

one web of life on Earth. The threads that come together in each of us stretch through time and space. The elements which make up your body now will have been part of trees, dinosaurs, mountains, flowers and tigers. They may have been in Gandhi or Hitler and will certainly have been part of lots of other people and animals over a vast span of time.

Tangible Levels of Connection

Human beings are profoundly social. We are born at an earlier stage of brain development than other mammals and so our early experience outside the womb profoundly shapes us. And so, for better or worse, we become attuned to our culture very early on. We have to. We need to connect in order to function as human beings. We exist in relationship with our families, our friends, our colleagues, our local community, our national society and the international community in tangible and intangible ways that affect every area of our lives.

For centuries we in the West have been caught in the assumption that we are separate from the environment around us and that we could therefore, without consequence, dominate and make use of it.

'Instead of seeing the environment as the foundation of human history, settled societies, especially modern industrial societies, have acted under the illusion that they are somehow independent from the natural world, which they have generally preferred to see as something apart, which they can exploit with more or less impunity.'

Clive Ponting, *A Green History of the World*

We are now in a paradigm shift. Systems thinking is becoming accepted in more and more academic disciplines as the new norm. Ecological awareness is becoming accepted both intellectually and practically. When the credit crunch affects everyone in the world who has any contact with money, when globalization of trade affects everyone who buys or sells anything, when climate change affects all of us and when the internet gives so many of us access to opinions and information, we have to acknowledge that we are in a new world, an interconnected world where citizens have more power than ever and where the idea that we can sustainably think or act as separate individuals or nations has bitten the dust.

Every time we turn on the tap, switch on the lights or the kettle or go shopping, we are involved in a very real and physical sense in a network of people, relationships and dynamics which stretch around the world. Through globalization, the clothes, food, toys, machines and other objects which have become central to our lives are now sourced and made all over the world. You may never go to India, but you probably drink tea grown there every day. You may never go to China, but a large proportion of your clothes is likely to have been made there.

Every consumer choice we make is a vote for one world or another. Do you support factory farming or free-range farming? Do you buy locally produced food or food that has been shipped thousands of miles? Do you know what you are saying 'yes' to with your 'consumer votes'? Our ignorance of how the goods we use are produced deprives us not just of the information with which we could make conscious choices as consumers, but also of a real and dynamic sense of how we are woven into the world and the world into us. Realizing our intimate connection with the web of life bestows on us the responsibility to use our consumer power consciously.

Susannah: *A few years ago we were busy flying about Europe with our work. An English couple called Chloë and Christian came to a workshop of ours in Switzerland by train. They told us how lovely it had been to arrive that way and why they had chosen it (to minimize the CO_2 their journey would produce). We logged it, but no more than that. It didn't seem relevant to us, as we had the idea that it was impossible for us to do what we wanted to and not fly.*

A while later Sue Rickards, a 5 Rhythms teacher who lives in London, extolled the virtues of travelling to Europe by train via the Channel Tunnel and said that she could no longer feel right about flying with the emissions being so high. That went in a little more.

A few more months later I met Jewls Wingfield, another movement teacher, on Totnes High Street and over a (Fairtrade) coffee she told me she had just decided not to fly any more. And she told me about an amazing website (www.seat61.com) which detailed how to get from the UK to anywhere in Europe by train.

That did it. We looked it up, and suddenly the impossible seemed both possible and necessary. Now we happily go by train most everywhere we go. Arriving for the first time in Paris by train, my body was so delighted that I did a jig down the rue! Such a relief to stay on the ground and still get there.

I'm telling this story because it reflects how slow we can be to change. Sometimes we need to hear something over and over again before we get it.

It was also so nice to learn about something we could do simply through our friends' happy example, rather than being told off or made to feel bad. We've come to relish our times on the train and find that we have wonderful conversations and get so much done, which is much harder on the plane and impossible in the car.

Your House

- **Intention:** To become more conscious of our tangible interconnectedness.

- **Purpose:** Through this consciousness, to become more awake to our choices.

Your house contains numerous proofs of our interconnectedness. What goods and food come in? Where do they come from in the world? Make a map.

Then choose one product to focus on. How is it produced? How do the people that are involved in making or growing it live and work? What are the effects on the environment and local community of how it is produced and then transported?

Where does your water come from?

What goes out of your house? Where does it go? Do you know where your household rubbish goes? Go and see the tip! Where does your sewage go? How much of what goes out can flow into the cycle of recycling and renewing, which planet Earth has depended on for millennia, and how much will be sealed in plastic bags for thousands of years?

The information your search reveals can be both a joy and a bit of a shock. Feel what you feel and then use that energy to act. What alternatives are there? Talk to the people you live with and decide what changes you would like to make. Remember, everything matters.

Caterpillar and
Butterfly Medicine

The ecological web of life on this planet pays no heed to national identity. If the oceans rise, they will not respect national boundaries either. We will sink or swim together. The challenges that we are facing today are bringing us slowly and surely to the understanding that we are one human family living in one common home.

Whilst it seems as if many structures that we once relied on are breaking down, there is the possibility that this breakdown is in fact a necessary process as we evolve in the consciousness of our interconnection. Elisabet Sahtouris, the well-known evolution biologist, has captured the idea perfectly:

> '*My favorite metaphor for the current world transition, first drawn to my attention by Norie Huddle, author of* Butterfly, *is that of a butterfly in metamorphosis. It goes like this:*
>   *Inside a cocoon, deep in the caterpillar's body, tiny things biologists call "imaginal disks" begin to form. Not recognizing the newcomers, the caterpillar's immune system snuffs them. But they keep coming faster and faster, then begin to link up with each other. Eventually the caterpillar's immune system fails from the stress and the disks become imaginal cells that build the butterfly from the meltdown of the caterpillar's body. If we see ourselves as imaginal discs working to build the butterfly of a better world, we will also see how important it is to link with each other in the effort, to recognize how many different kinds of imaginal cells it will take to build a butterfly with all its capabilities and colors.*'

So far, we have resisted acknowledging and acting from our mutual need for sustainable life on Earth. But now our interconnectedness is tangible and apparent to us all. We cannot escape our shared destiny. But here, maybe, is the hope in the crisis that we have brought on ourselves. Climate change, along with concurrent species and habitat extinction, pollution and food and water shortages, has become a strong evolutionary adaptive pressure for us to make a quantum jump into a way of seeing, thinking, feeling and acting which acknowledges that life on Earth is one family.

Widening the Connection

Connection makes us what we are. And we want to belong. This is both a gift and a challenge. We tend to identify with a group, or a culture, or a nation, and think of those outside as 'other'. And often we strengthen our sense of belonging by making that 'other' appear as an opposite, often a negative opposite. This 'tribalism' and tendency to split into factions seems to be a pretty generic feature of the human make-up. One can imagine how, when we were hunter-gatherers, it served its purpose in splitting up groups which had grown too big to be sustainable, but now we share a common destiny. Can we make the shift to forming a caring bond with all life on Earth?

At the time of writing, there is still war raging in so many places on this Earth. Iron fists and the politics of revenge upon revenge are squeezing the hope and the life out of so many thousands of people. Isn't it time that we grew up? To take revenge is nothing new. To act with cruelty is nothing new. To allow our own unconsciousness to dictate our actions and to create and recreate the very things we are afraid of is nothing new. Isn't it time that we looked beyond ourselves and worked to create the conditions of social justice, respect for diversity and for the environment and spiritual fulfilment that would truly give peace a chance? What will it take for us to stand up and to realize that we are indeed brothers and sisters?

Unity, Freedom and Interconnection in the Dance

Susannah: *Several years ago I was involved in a rite of passage project for teenage girls called 'Maiden Voyage'. We went to the island of La Gomera in the Canaries to dance, write and see the wild dolphins. When we went out on the boat into the wide blue space of the sea, the skipper said that it was not a matter of us finding the dolphins, but of them finding us, if they wanted to. He thought that what the dolphins responded to was not so much the consciousness of the individuals on the boat, but the level of connectedness between them.*

The girls I was with had laughed and wept, shared vulnerability and strength, ceremony and challenge together. The dolphins liked them. At one point there were dolphins coming towards the small boat from literally all around us. The skipper said he had never seen so many come or stay for so long with one boat. From the far horizon, from the middle horizon and from close by, they leapt towards us. The power! It was almost scary. And then they played. Dolphins were swimming by themselves, in pairs, in threesomes and in groups, leaping out of the waves in unison. At one point a large group 'stood up' in lines, their tails waggling as if they were waving to us. I was laughing, crying, engulfed in gratitude that these wild

*joyous creatures of the sea should choose to share their
play with us.*

*To me, it looked as if each individual dolphin was
weaving its own seamless melody line, always aware of
the others but always connected to itself. As a dancer,
I was inspired. I imagined being on a dance floor with
everyone free, following their own thread and seamlessly
moving between dancing solo, with a partner, with small
groups, with larger groups and with the whole group – a
spontaneous mix of unity and freedom, individuality and
community.*

*I have worked with this dream for a while in workshops
and when the 'dolphin grace' arrives, as it does more
and more frequently, I feel the joy in surfing on the edge
between 'me' and 'we', between form and formlessness.
No wonder dolphins seem so happy!*

This level of combined freedom and awareness is rare. Most
of us, most of the time, seem to rely either on conformity
or on a separate sort of individuality. This apparent polarity
between the individual and the collective mirrors a dilemma
of our times. We want to belong without the cost of sacrificing
our truth and we want to be ourselves without the loneliness
it so often implies. To be free *and* connected means feeling
vulnerable, available, exposed, no longer immune to each
other, no longer able to hide by being in control or under
control. It means finding an acceptance of the unknown,
the unpredictable flux between form and formlessness, the
dynamic interplay between ourselves and the world. It means
taking responsibility for ourselves, assuming the authority to
lead and finding the willingness to follow. And it means finding
a fusion between the 'individualism' of the West and the 'group
mind' of the East.

The biggest criticism that we hear of people on the personal
growth path is that they become more and more self-centred.

This is because when we start to get free, the first part of our plerk (play + work = plerk) is often a release and expression of ourselves. We have both experienced this necessary station on the journey of waking up. Without doubt, asking 'Who am I and what do I need?' is an important first question on the path, but it is only the first question. We need to address it and move on. There is a saying: 'Find yourself, that's half the way to God. Then lose yourself and all the way is trod.' So the next question is: 'Can I take my new-found sense of self and let it grow into a bigger realm?'

Susannah: *As each person discovers how to follow their own dance and to become conscious of the whole, the grounds for co-creation are established. It's as if we all have an energetic umbrella. The stalk of the umbrella is your presence within yourself, your trunk. The umbrella itself is the spread of your awareness of the space and field around you. Once your stalk is firmly established, you can open your umbrella. If everyone in a room is doing this, the umbrellas can merge and a group consciousness can emerge which does not subordinate the individual intelligences but grows out of their linking.*

Then magic starts to happen. Spontaneous theatre, choreography, dance forms and movement 'rituals' emerge without thinking or planning. The spark that sets it all alight might come from anywhere – we are all free to ignite it. As a man we knew called Roy said to us a long time ago: 'Freedom with awareness – that's liberation.'

It seems to us that at this point in human evolution we need all the resources we can collectively muster. If we are all to make our creativity and inspiration available to the world and if we are all to work together as individuals and nations, we need to nourish the qualities of fluidity, confidence, listening and connectedness. The dance floor is a wonderful place to practise these skills and experience interconnection.

Intangible Levels of Connection

Because everything has its energy which affects everything else, we are connected not just by our actions, but by our thoughts, feelings and prayers as well. We're sure you have had those experiences of thinking of a friend and then they ring, or of dreaming of someone and finding that your dream had accuracy. Put negatively, as a psychic once told us, 'A curse is simply somebody thinking badly of you.' When we heard this, it reminded us of Tony Robbins's powerful suggestion to practise assuming the best of people.

In our experience, those we have loved stay forever in our hearts. And our thoughts and feelings about those we know and love (and more than likely those we don't) are felt through time and space.

Ya'Acov: *Susannah, our son and I were living in our first house in south Devon, a beautiful big-roomed high-ceilinged place. One night we were all at home when my mother called to tell me that Grandma Jean had had another stroke and that she might not make it through the night. Though there had been many of these situations before, I immediately had a very strong sense that indeed she would die in the night and I told my mum that if she could, she should go and be with her. I told her that I would pray for her.*

I explained to Susannah what was happening and said that I was going to do a little ceremony for my grandma. I went into the large living room, put on some waltz music, lit a candle, drew the large pale blue curtains and turned the lights off. In my imagination I started to dance slowly with my grandmother. I felt her presence very strongly. I talked to her as we danced. I reminded her of all the beautiful things and memories she would leave behind. I talked to her about the times I'd stayed with her and how I'd loved the smell of toast and marmalade that would be the first thing I smelled in the mornings. I thanked her for giving birth to my mum and my uncle. I danced and talked with her for over an hour, me in Devon and her in Southport, 300 miles between us and yet not an inch. I felt her fear of dying. I thanked her again and again for the love she had given all of us and for the life she'd lived. I prayed to everything I knew to make her passage safe and as painless as possible.

At a certain point, the wind rattled our old windows, the candle flickered and went out and I said goodbye.

My grandmother died peacefully in her sleep that night. Though we all grieved her passing, there was a feeling that the time had been right for her to go.

Two years later I was in Edinburgh. I had been teaching at the weekend and had the Monday morning free to stroll around the beautiful old city and to do a little window-shopping. A fine misty rain was falling and I was tired and feeling lazy and delightfully aimless.

Following my nose up and down the hills of the city, looking for those narrow streets where all the hidden jewels of the city lie in wait for those who seek, I spotted a funky-looking clothes stall offering street wear and mountain wear with lots of labels stitched in interesting patterns, and pockets and buttons galore. I crossed the street to take a closer look, but somehow I must have walked through the

wrong doorway, because as I shook the rain off myself,
I realized that I was in one of the shabbiest offices I had
ever been in. The upholstery was old, dust and cobwebs
were everywhere, calendars from years past were taped
over peeling wallpaper and half-open filing cabinets were
cluttering up the space. Behind the desk, which was strewn
with papers and dirty coffee cups, sat a slight old lady with
silver-blond hair. She wore a white embroidered cardigan
and had a small gold Star of David round her neck. She had
kind eyes, and in front of her, on the only clear bit of desk,
was a red diary open on the day's date. It looked to be full
of appointments.

I stammered a rather strange question: 'Where am I?
Only I was looking for the clothes shop...'

'Oh no, dear,' she replied in a soft Edinburgh brogue,
'the clothes shop is next door. You are in the office of the
foremost psychic in Scotland, Mr, well Reverend is more
accurate, Beadley, but I'm sorry, dear, the Reverend has no
space for appointments for the next six weeks. You'll have
to book and come back.'

I told her that I wasn't looking for a psychic, but thanked
her anyway and prepared to go next door.

I was just reaching for the door handle, when she piped
up again, bright and enthusiastic: 'Er, excuse me, dear,
you may think that I am kidding you, but looking in my little
red book I can see that he has had a cancellation. There's a
slot available in 20 minutes. I suggest you take it.'

I turned round, feeling a little sceptical, but her eyes
were telling me the truth, so I accepted the offer. I paid
my 20 quid and sat down in a sagging armchair to wait.
I was curious and a little nervous. It felt as if something
indefinable had guided me there. It was almost as if I was
in a dream.

After around a quarter of an hour, a man with tear-
streaked eyes came through the door to the right. He was

wearing a heavy overcoat and looked as though he was leaving a funeral. He was soon followed by, unmistakably, the 'Reverend' Beadley. He was enormous, wore spectacles and had the kind of blotchy red skin that comes from eating too much red meat and drinking too much red wine. Sporting a dirty white dog collar and a big fat belly, he was quite a presence. I stood up to greet him.

'Don't say a word, young man.' He had a heavy Yorkshire accent. 'People like to test me, and I find it better that they say nothing at all. Follow me.'

He led the way into his reading room, which made the front office seem positively palatial in comparison. Sitting down behind his desk, he took a wrapped black cassette out of one of the drawers and tested an old cassette recorder to make sure it was working. 'I like to record the sessions, so you can remember what happens here today. Ready to begin, lad?'

I nodded, barely suppressing my laughter at this surreal situation I had walked into, but soon he had my full attention as he launched into a 20-minute monologue about my personal history. He gave me names, places, events, wounds, successes, the whole lot, and all with quite stunning accuracy.

What happened next will stay with me forever. 'I don't normally do this, lad, but I think it will be fine with you. I'm getting a knock from the other side, if you know what I mean. Yes, I can see her now, a tiny woman, blonde hair, graceful, your mother's mother, I think. She's smiling at you. She's holding out a record for you, classical waltz music by the looks of it. She just wants to say, "Thanks for dancing with me on the night I died."'

My dam burst. I let go and wept with enormous gratitude to spirit for guiding me to this most unlikely angel. Like the tall man before me, I left that little dusty haven in the city with my eyes still streaming tears.

Out in the rain again, the grey streets had a new shine to them. Everything did. I whistled my way back to the hotel with my grandmother's love and support all around me.

However it was that this extraordinary man gave this gift to Ya'Acov, it gave both of us the feeling of how interconnected we truly are – even, it seems, beyond this mortal coil.

For All our Relations

- **Intention:** To connect with the energetic worldwide web of life.

- **Purpose:** To strengthen our experience of interconnectedness and send out blessings.

This mediation is good to do alone or with friends.

In your work space, do whatever you need to do to come to stillness. Then sit down, with your spine vertical and your legs as symmetrical as possible. Use a cushion if you need to and make sure you are comfortable. Letting your tail drop, feeling it rooting downwards energetically and letting the crown of your head rise to the heavens, feel your spine elongate gently. Spread your chest wide and give breathing space to your heart. Feel your whole body breathing and let the energy of your heart soften, widen and deepen in the breathing space of the body. Take a moment to feel the love and support of the Earth beneath you and the sun above you. Breathe it in.

If you are doing this with friends, take their hands and feel the connection spreading from you to them.

Then extend your awareness to include your immediate family, friends, neighbours and companions and send them warmth and blessings that today and all the days of their lives will be good ones.

Keep expanding now, feeling love and sending out blessings to your community, the land where you live and your country.

Expand more now to include the animal, mineral and plant worlds, the world of your ancestors and the unseen world of spirit.

Send your love, blessings and gratitude out in an ever-expanding circle. Keep breathing and expanding until you can see, in your mind's eye, the beauty of this blue-green jewel of a planet as if from space.

You may find yourself becoming aware of both the exuberant life force and the suffering on Earth. Spread the wings of your heart wide and see if you can make space to witness the joy and the sorrow together.

Imagine a light shining from your heart like another sun shining on the Earth. As you do this, imagine many thousands of beating hearts on Earth all practising this meditation at the same time. Each heart is like another sun and as you witness this, you recognize that the same light that shines through your heart is shining through every heart on Earth. You experience directly this feeling of unity and interconnection.

Find a way to salute or thank the spirit of life on Earth as it moves through you and all things. At this moment, you don't have to fix it or imagine it all healed. Just hold the Earth in your hands and let your love and gratitude flow towards and through it. Maybe you want to dance or sing or sit silently as you send prayers for all your relations.

> When you feel ready, gently come back to your own space and your own body and go on with your day, allowing this sense of interconnectedness to fuse your thoughts and feelings and actions.

Once you experience the web of life as a living, breathing diverse and beautiful whole, it is difficult not to love it, want to protect it, cherish it and sustain it. The willingness to experience this connectedness involves a willingness to feel it and to share in its strength and fragility, its sorrow and its joy.

Susannah: *As I lay on the earth on my soft blanket, the fire warming my face, I felt like a kitten curled up, in divine rest on my mother's breast. The earth energy filled me up, flooding me with softness. I felt my lungs opening, and with that, a great relief and soft weeping as I recognized a deep level of separation I had felt from life.*

The sorrow kept growing, waves of tears washing through me as I lay, belly down now, on the ground. I saw the pale ghosts of the vicious circles of pain we inflict on each other, over and over, on and on, until all I could do was howl, flinging my anguish bursting like fireworks into the dark, quiet night sky. The guide who was accompanying me sat quietly by the fire, playing a mournful, gentle tune.

And then I saw the pale green soft young leaves of a small tree which was growing close by. Translucent in the firelight, they shone with the naked life pouring through them. With the shining green leaves of this little beech tree softly anointing my eyes, I found myself in a place of love, awe and reverence. And I saw how the capacity to harm anything or anyone is linked to disconnection and that this separation is possible because we have anaesthetised ourselves from life. To recover our senses, to recover our hearts, to recover our connectedness, we have to be willing to feel. The heart that is anaesthetized against its own pain is anaesthetized full stop. Coming out from the dull sleepwalk of numbed existence means being willing to feel the agony as well as the ecstasy. We are all in need of healing.

The experience of interconnection is a major part of Living the Dream. To know ourselves as part of something bigger and to have a sense of working together towards a dream is one of the most satisfying dances we can be involved in. When each of us is empowered to give of the best of ourselves, then the rainbow we are part of, far from being some pastel façade of awakening, becomes a vibrant and dynamic bridge of hope across the stormy skies.

As high as an experience this undoubtedly is, there is one more step to take. And to take it, we have to be willing to let go altogether. Let's dance over the page and into the final gateway of the Movement Medicine mandala, Realization.

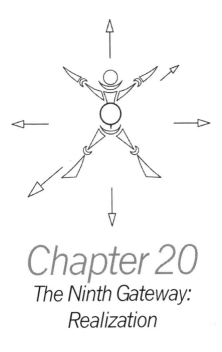

Chapter 20
The Ninth Gateway:
Realization

*'Darkness cannot drive out darkness,
only light can do that.
Hate cannot drive out hate,
only love can do that.'*

Martin Luther King

Welcome to the ninth gateway, and congratulations for making it here! This is the gateway of Realization. According to the dictionary, 'realization' is 'the act of becoming fully aware of something as a fact'. Though faith is a powerful state, direct experience is the source of knowledge. For someone to tell you that you are loved, or indeed, that you are love, is one thing. To experience it for yourself is another.

A Full-Spectrum Existence

In the eighth gateway we can experience the joy of being part of a unified whole through being who we are and making our contribution. In the ninth gateway, we are invited to take the next step and directly experience the oneness of all of creation.

Our friend Jake, writing about his own experience of a process called the Enlightenment Intensive in his book *Tell Me Who You Are*, puts it like this:

> *'So you persist – you carry on, and after a while you see it – the beautiful crystal palace. OOOOOH!! This is too much – oh wow! This is absolutely divine – oh! I never imagined anything could be so beautiful. You just stare in awe. You go up to the Master and say: "I've seen it – and it's so beautiful, I never knew." And he will say – now get inside it. There is still a separation between you and it – between you and what you are seeing. Remember that what you want is a direct experience of the Truth – a state of no separation.'*

To experience the oneness of all of creation is a radical moment. It changes your view and gives a new context and perspective to the rest of your life. It's not an experience that appears on demand. There are 10,000 methods of getting there and yet it is the ultimate paradox that, once there, the stunning realization that is widely reported in despatches from those graced enough to have visited, is that there is nothing one can do to reach this state. Why? Because it already exists, eternally and everywhere, and it seems to be as simple as opening your eyes.

In the Movement Medicine mandala, this ninth gateway is the Gateway of White Light. Just as the full spectrum of the rainbow is contained in white light, so all the other gateways are contained within the experiences that this gateway offers. White light itself is the force that illuminates everything, including those things we would rather lay hidden. It is the eternal heart of everything that lives and the gateway to the infinite mystery beyond.

For us, realization is a twofold dance. First, there is the experience of being white light or universal love and peace or the wave becoming the ocean or the many other poetic names for the experience. Second, there is the achievement of what we like to call 'full-spectrum living'. If you refract white light with a crystal you get the full spectrum of colour. In the reverse process, if you omit any colour, you don't get white light. If all the colours are there, they disappear into light which is itself invisible and at the same time contains and illuminates everything – simultaneously nothing and everything.

Like the American expression 'to go the whole nine yards', a full-spectrum existence means to live your life with a full awareness of and engagement with all 9 Gateways and all the colours of the rainbow.

It's All about Love

Throughout the time and space of human existence, people the world over have stretched the very limits of their imaginations to try to convey the experience of the dissolution of the separate self and the profound experience of love it engenders.

Love is the key. It doesn't matter where we travel, or where we look, or what path we're on. In the end, it all comes down to the same thing: it's the power of love, the feeling that just won't be suppressed or strait-jacketed, that makes it all worth it in this human dance.

Love is the guidance system we are given to help us find our way in this life. And it is the most unpredictable and fascinating of all dances. Just when you think you've pinned it down and understood it, it'll turn around, drop its form like an old skin and emerge backwards and upside down to confound you. Love is waiting for us on every journey and around every corner. It's singing to us with every sunrise and speaking to us through the sunset colours in the sky and the scent of night flowers on the wind. It's there inside the blood, as ancient as the first breath and as fresh as a first kiss. Love lifts our noses out of our own belly buttons and shows us that we are part of something bigger than ourselves. It's a telegram from the Creator that sometimes gently rocks us and sometimes totally shocks us out of our apathy. It offers us a new view and the power to dream. It reminds us of what is important to us and what we are here for. It exists beyond us and yet we are made from it.

Without love, life is a brittle and dry version of itself. And yet, love is always present. It is the bringer of hope and is the one thing in all the world that can transform and heal even the most desperate of wounds and the most wretched of situations. Love is the Great Healer.

You Are Loved

The first realization in this ninth gateway is that we are all loved. Whether we feel it or not is another thing entirely. But your body, your heart and your mind are gifts of love. Your past, your present and your future are gifts of love. And your fulfilment and our interconnection are gifts of love too. The breath you are breathing, the sun that will rise in the morning, the Earth turning beneath you, the force of attraction that keeps atoms and molecules and planets and galaxies spinning in an eternal dance of evolution, all these are gifts of love. That you can choose the meaning of your life, that you are free to act and react in your own unique way, and that you can take great leaps of faith and choose the unexpected path are enormous and everyday gifts from this creative force of the universe. And this force is both within you and beyond you.

There are many ways to strengthen the knowledge that you are loved. 'The 21 Gratitudes' meditation helps us to recognize what we are receiving. Another of the very best ways we have found is to spend a little time writing yourself a letter from the Creator or from your own highest self.

A Letter from the Creator

- **Intention:** To contact the love that creation has for you in a very direct and personal way.

- **Purpose:** To realize that you are loved and that this consciousness is within you.

Create a quiet and peaceful space. Light a candle; dance if you want to. When you are ready, alone or with friends, ask the creative source within you to write you a letter to help you to experience how deeply loved you are right now. We are certain you will be amazed by what comes through you.

When you get to the end, ask for a PS about what this source specifically values in you, for instance:

- 'I value your passionate and gentle heart.'

- 'I value your chutzpah and your humility.'

> - 'I value your delightful sense of humour.'
> - 'I value your love of life.'
>
> If you are doing this with friends, take time to read your letters to each other. To witness each other in this kind of space and to shine the light of the love you feel for your friends freely on each other will only serve to enhance this experience and the realization that you are loved.

You Are Love

Knowing that you are loved is a blessing. Knowing that in the deepest and most essential place within you all is one and that you *are* that love is a trip to Shangri-La. It is ecstasy. And paradoxically, it can become the most ordinary and everyday state.

Dance has always been one of the most direct routes to trance and ecstatic states of oneness, from rave culture to sun dances, from ceremonies in the forests of Gabon to trance dance workshops the world over. Movement Medicine is but one of the many practices that humans have developed to facilitate a safe journey there and back again.

Ecstasy is the experience of the dynamic interplay between finding our true expression and the total surrender of our separate sense of self. We find a true sense of self in the dance and then, every now and again, the dance itself invites us to let go and fall into her arms. Since the very first drumbeat, human beings have been creating environments where they can experience this simple and profound sense of individuality, unity and dissolution.

Ecstasy is catalytic in a very real sense. It reminds us of a deeper world, a world where movement is the physical language of the soul, a world where the soul speaks to us in a spontaneous and idiosyncratic unfolding of the dreams we each bring with us to manifest in this world. And, most importantly, a world where we remember the ease of being the Eternal Self we have always been, unique and simultaneously connected to everything around us.

Ecstatic states create a flow of generosity and empathy. Imagine a room full of people in a similar state and you will begin to get the flavour of what this is all about. Imagine this and the true meaning of the word 'ecstasy' starts to hum with the promise of spirit and matter in unison.

Everybody feels it when it happens. You can't fake it. It's delicious. The lights turn out and there is a glow emanating from the dancers. They are pure movement, as outrageous and spontaneous as creation itself. When the circle or community is strong and the other dancers present are awake and sensitive to their environment, all can benefit from the experience of the one. And inside the dance, the dancer is simply taken away and stripped of the illusion of a separate identity.

Ya'Acov: *There was blood, sweat and tears. I danced and yet I wasn't there. Stories were told through this body, heartbreaking stories, inspiring stories, as the dance stretched me out on the endless void between light and dark, between the living and the dead. And all the time there was an absolute awareness of these feet dancing, these brothers and sisters, the walls of the studio, the trees and the city streets outside.*

Once that veil has been lifted, life is never the same. Our circumstances may be the same, but our relationship to them has been altered forever. However hard the understudy self tries to reassert its hold over the body, heart and mind, the dancer inside knows the power they have to dance past the ongoing limitations of personal history. We have remembered the power of letting go. We have gained the ability to become our own healers and to retrieve and embody the soul. All the aspects of our soul which been fragmented hear the echoes of this new life and want to return. And we know, without words, that as surely as the ocean is connected to the moon, we are connected, we are one and we are the power of love.

There is no recipe for this realization. It can come anytime and anywhere. It is beyond dogma or creed. And it is beyond our control. But somewhere between being and doing, somewhere between the words and the notes, the truth of who we are is waiting for us to turn around, look into the mirror of infinite love and recognize ourselves staring back.

The realization that we are loved and that we are love and that it is our task to embody this truth on Earth in our own unique way is the essence of the 9 Gateways of Movement Medicine.

The Reality of Mortality

Many people talk about the moment of letting go as being like dying. Indeed, in spiritual pathways the world over we hear again and again of the importance of 'dying whilst we are still living'. On our own journeys, we have been introduced to Death as the Great Teacher. In one ceremony, we were invited to dig our own graves and were then 'buried' as shamans held a funeral for our recently departed souls. We were invited to spend the night in dialogue with Death to look back over our lives with Death as a guide. Were we at peace with our lives? Had we given everything that we came to give? Had we left any loose ends untied or relationships incomplete? As the dawn approached, we had to 'make a deal with Death'. We were to ask Death to give us another year and to make an agreement about how we would live our lives if we were to be given a second chance. What was truly important to us? We were invited to make pledges about how we would choose to live our lives with the knowledge that our time here was finite.

What a difference those ceremonies made to our lives and to how we felt about dying. The reality of our mortality is a very important realization indeed. To have Death as a friendly presence in our lives, who every now and again reminds us of our pledges, has been a great benefit.

Karl Rechtenbacher was a man who had a visionary spirit. With his partner Gabriele, his son Zackes, his company Fire Performance Group Nachtwerk and later on as a member of the Action Theatre PanOptikum, he worked tirelessly to manifest his vision for many years. He created spectacular emotional open-air theatre, including song, music, fire and acrobatics. Eventually the PanOptikum productions began to gain recognition and the company began to get major funding. Then Karl discovered that he had cancer. According to the doctors there was a 97 per cent certainty he had no more than three to four months to live. He was advised to start chemotherapy instantly, but he decided to look for an alternative way of healing instead. He was convinced that he only had a chance of fighting his cancer if he was ready to face it on a physical, emotional and spiritual level. Supported by his family and his friends, he started to work intensively with homoeopathic doctors, Family Constellations therapy, alternative diet advisers and a Gestalt therapist, with whom he focused on the unresolved conflicts of his life.

Two months after he started this intense inner work, he died. However, through this process he completed himself and found something deep that he wasn't aware of before his sickness. On the last morning of his life, now very weak, he entered a beatific space in which he seemed to shine from inside with a deep peacefulness. At one point, he said to Gabriele: 'That which holds together the whole universe is unalterable, irrefutable, indestructible, unconditional, absolute *love*. You can't do anything about it! Did you understand? Do you understand?!'

When we heard these words from Gabriele, they hit a chord and they have stayed with us ever since. We want to share them with you and to honour Karl's visionary spirit and courage. And we say a big thank you to Gabriele Pekusa and Zackes Brustik for their permission to include Karl's story.

Meeting Death as an Ally

- **Intention:** To ask Death to be your teacher and guide as you live your life.

- **Purpose:** To realize the finite amount of time you have to further realize the preciousness of this life.

Go to your work space and wake up and align your body, heart and mind with movement practice.

When you are ready, ask what we learnt to call 'Benevolent Death' to come and visit you and teach you more about life. Invite Death to sit down with you and dialogue with you.

Try to be very ordinary about the whole thing. Acknowledge your fears, if you have them, and ask Death to help you to look at your life through their eyes.

- If you were to die today, would you die peacefully, content with how you had lived your life? If not, why not?

- Do you have any unfinished business with friends, family or colleagues?

- Are there dreams that you have given up on prematurely?

- If you knew you only had one more year to live, is there anything about your life you would change?

Feel free to free write down the answers to these questions.

Ask Death if they have any advice for you before they leave.

Do you wish to make any pledges to Death? This is a serious matter and we strongly recommend that you only make pledges that you know you will do your absolute utmost to keep.

If you want to, ask Death to be a teacher and guide for you and to help you to make the most of life whilst you are still living. When you are ready, thank them for coming and let them go.

We suggest that it would be good to dance a while now to thoroughly enjoy the feeling of life moving through you. If you have made pledges, it is a very good to take the first step on the road to fulfilling them right away.

Peace

Ya'Acov: *When I was seven, I wanted to be a rabbi. I was in love with the mystery of life. Each night, I would fall asleep the same way. I loved this private time at the end of each day. I would lie there saying thank you for the day* *and once I'd done, I would settle back and ask my little body to relax. I don't know where this meditation came from. Maybe I brought it with me. I would lie back and start to enjoy my breathing. I would feel the weight of my body sinking into the bed and the feeling I knew so well would slowly come back to me and I would start to expand. In my mind, I grew until I embraced the room, the house with all my family in it, the street, the neighbourhood, the town, country, continent, world and everything in it. I would keep going until I could feel the moon and I felt as if my thumbs could tickle the stars. I would go out past the sun, and when I'd gone just as far as my mind could reach, I would wait there, ecstatic, expectant, letting this whole expanded sense of self fill up with a feeling of immense peace. I fell into its awesome vast blackness each and every night for years and years. I was never alone there. I disappeared, and everything I knew or worried about or cared about disappeared too. I was so safe there, because I was no longer. At the same time, it was the most intense experience of being and each night I fell over the edge of myself into the arms of peace.*

Much more recently, I saw a video of a talk given by neuro-anatomist Jill Bolte Taylor at a conference. With great courage, humour and intelligence, she described the extraordinary experience of being the witness to her own stroke. Her left brain slowly ground to a halt and catapulted her into the pure expanded consciousness of her right brain. Every now and again, her left brain would kick into gear again and insist that she needed to act to save her life before she fell over the edge of herself again into what she amusingly called 'La La Land'. I cried listening to her so beautifully and eloquently describing the experiences of my early years. She survived her stroke and came back with the passionate intention of reminding as many of us as possible of our capacity to experience this oneness with all of life.

If we follow any question deeply enough, we will arrive in the same place of mystery. And the Great Mystery is actually a source of peace. In the end, perhaps the deepest realization of all is the realization of peace.

There is nothing new about peace, oneness and love. They are realizations as old as the hills. And love is a force to be reckoned with. To feel how hurt we are and how angry we are is one thing. To act from that place in our relationships as individuals and as nations will only serve to continue the hurt. If the millions of individuals who have experienced the ultimate truth that we are one are right, then if I hurt you, I am hurting myself. It is as simple as that.

So how do we put peace into the world? The only ways we know are: 1) to cultivate peace within us, between us and around us, and 2) to find the strength and the courage to listen to, respect and work with those who have a different way from us. For us, peace is not just about sitting quietly in a lotus position and beaming out good vibes into the world – it is also a passionate affair that involves the celebration of diversity and the joyful task of bringing a little peace into the world through our actions. Our final recipe is one that is close to our hearts.

Throw a Peace Party

- **Intention:** To make space for yourself and your community to experience the peace that comes from dancing your socks off.

- **Purpose:** To put peace into the world through your being and through raising money to support peace projects.

Why not get together with your friends and organize a 'Peace Party'? Throw a party that celebrates the diversity of life on Earth and celebrates peace as a passionate state worth living for. Why not make it a charitable event that raises money for any one of the hundreds of projects that are working to bring peace and reconciliation to situations of war or conflict? At the School of Movement Medicine we run these dances regularly, so if you want to find a little inspiration, look up the next dance and we'll see you there.

It's a big job to create a great party space. You can either do this as a 'friends only' (and friends of friends) event or do a public gig, which is more complicated. For that, you need insurance and entertainment licences, and there's a whole bunch of other stuff to think about too. So we suggest simply finding the next good excuse to party for peace and inviting your friends. If you're celebrating a birthday, why not ask your friends to donate something to your chosen projects rather than buying you things that you may not need?

Get together a team to support you if necessary. You'll need a good venue where noise isn't a problem, good lighting, good décor to create an atmosphere, a good sound system and good DJs who know how to create a great vibe with their music. For public events you'll also need good publicity and stewards to guide people where necessary. A chai and fresh juice stand helps, and we always like to decorate the space in accordance with the theme, including having an installation in the centre of the room with all four elements present. If you're raising money for a particular project, it's great to have information available for your guests to show them where their gift is going.

Let your guests know that the intention of the party is to put a little more peace into the world and tell them that they are invited to come and dance themselves through all their worries and concerns. Remember the sense of peace that comes from totally letting go!

It helps to have a moment, maybe towards the end of the party, where you invite everyone to come together and focus all the great energy you've gathered on creating peace in the world. This can happen in the dance or you can create a still point. Meditation is no longer as far out as it used to be, so have courage and ask your friends to support you.

Don't underestimate the power the dance has to encourage everyone who attends to deepen their commitment to bringing forward change and evolution in our world. And who knows, you may disappear in the dance for a while and slip through the infinite gateway of Realization.

And once you've begun, who knows where it will end? Enjoy!

So where to from here? We've travelled through the 9 Gateways to Living your Dream and if you've done your work, you are no doubt on the way. What's next?

It's time to take another ride. From the realization of oneness, we bring our experiences back to Earth and continue with the realignment of body, heart and mind. We continue to honour our past and our ancestors, be in the present and keep working to co-create the future. And we go on with the never-ending journey of fulfilment, interconnection and realization. This is full-spectrum living, and round and round the spiral we dance, each journey a new ring on the Tree of Life. And each journey brings a little more wisdom, a lot more passion for what we do and more of a sense of humour about ourselves. As we deepen our practice, we discover again the natural innocence of having nothing to hide and the profound contentment of knowing who we are and what we are here to give. Like the universe itself, it's an endless and eternal dance.

⋯•• Part V •••⋯

Conclusion

Chapter 21
No More Excuses – Time to Live the Dream!

'Can we rely on it that a "turning around" will be accomplished by enough people quickly enough to save the modern world? This question is often asked, but whatever answer is given to it will mislead. The answer "yes" would lead to complacency; the answer "no", to despair. It is desirable to leave these perplexities behind us and get down to work.'

E. F. Schumacher

There are those who say that the suffering we inflict on Earth is just human nature. And there are those who say that we make agreements to love and to hate and to play out the full drama of human existence so that we can learn all about the light and the dark and evolve the soul. And there are those who believe that our time on Earth allows us the opportunity to consciously choose the love that is our deepest nature. There are some who believe that the universe is ultimately benevolent. There are others who believe it is implacably neutral. In this universe, it seems as if everything is true!

For us the simple truth is that we love the extraordinary beauty and diversity of life on Earth and we see how our current ways of living endanger it. So we have chosen to do our best to participate in bringing forth a world of sustainability and peace which confers meaning, healing and joy on the present and offers the future a chance. We hold in our hearts both the beauty that is present here and now and the vision of what a collective consciousness of oneness could create.

Maybe we are not spiritually evolved enough to be able to let go of our attachment to peace and humanity prevailing in this world. But it is how we are and it is, for the moment, who we are. We are happy with the choice we have made to dedicate our lives to the dream of bringing heaven to Earth. And we feel that this is a dream that is growing in many hearts and in many places around the world. Movement Medicine is one of many ways. It works for us. And we hope it offers some insight and something of value to you.

This is our offering and we make it in the full realization that it is not *the* truth, it is simply our truth. And since truth is a dancer too, we fully expect it to change.

Someone once told us that the only reason that the ancient Mayans wrote things down was so that they could be empty enough to receive the next 'instructions'. So as we go off to continue to dance our socks off and await our next instructions, we will leave you with a few questions:

- What is your truth?

- Do you want to live your dream?

- Do you want to be able to look in the mirror and love the person who is looking back at you? Will you?

- Do you want to take the steps from idea to action to manifestation? Will you?

- Do you want to be part of creating a new paradigm here on Earth – a paradigm that will leave a legacy of courageous actions taken based on seeing our own lives in the bigger picture?

- Do you choose to become empowered, responsible and live the dream you came here to live? Or do you choose to sleepwalk through these critical times, burying your head in excuses from the past and a whole bunch of distractions in the present?

- You are living a dream. Is it the one you came here to live?

We know how much courage it takes to find both the strength and the humility to take this journey. And we have seen thousands of people just like you make that choice. We have witnessed them taking the quantum leap from feeling like victims of circumstances to becoming co-creators. We have seen thousands of people of all shapes, sizes and ages who were living in the certainty that they couldn't dance, find a poise, grace and raw power in their movements that has spilled over from the dance floor into their lives.

So it really is up to you. This is your life. This is your dream. The dance floor of life is yours. And the dancer in you is waiting for your permission to lead you onto it.

We'll look forward to meeting you somewhere out there in the big unknown on the dance to who knows where. Now, stop, take a deep breath, and make a moment for peace.

Until we meet again, whoever you are, all power to you and your dreams.

One Love. 21 Gratitudes.

Ya'Acov & Susannah, 2009

Bibliography

Sandra Blakeslee and Matthew Blakeslee, *The Body Has a Mind of Its Own*, Random House, 2007

Joseph Campbell, *Myths to Live By*, Viking Press, 1972

Carlos Castaneda, *The Teachings of Don Juan: A Yaqui Way of Knowledge*, Penguin Books, 1970

Eva Chapman, *Sasha and Olga*, Lothian Books, 2006

Jake Chapman, *Tell Me Who You Are*, J. and E. Chapman in association with SPA, 1988

Antonio R. Damasio, *Descarte's Error: Emotion, Reason and the Human Brain*, Grosset/Putnam, 1994

Barbara Ehrenreich, *Dancing in the Streets: A History of Collective Joy*, Metropolitan Books, 2007

Fynn, *Mister God, This is Anna*, William Collin Sons and Co. Ltd, 1974

Sue Gerhardt, *Why Love Matters*, Routledge, 2004

Chloë Goodchild, *The Naked Voice*, Trafalgar Square, 1993

Temple Grandin, *Animals in Translation*, Bloomsbury, 2005

Jay Griffiths, *Wild*, Penguin Books, 2006

Bert Hellinger, Gabriele Ten Heovel and Colleen Beaumont, *Acknowledging What Is: Conversations with Bert Hellinger*, Zeig, Tucker & Theisen, 1999

Ray Hunt, *Think Harmony with Horses*, Pioneer Publishing Company, 1995

Steven Johnson, *Mind Wide Open*, Penguin Books, 2005

Jack Kornfield, *After the Ecstasy, the Laundry*, Rider, 2000

Elisabeth Kübler-Ross, *The Wheel of Life: A Memoir of Living and Dying*, Touchstone Books, 1998

Ursula K. Le Guin, *The Wizard of Earthsea*, Bantam Books, 1975

Peter Levine, *Waking the Tiger*, North Atlantic Books, 1997

Caryn McHose and Kevin Frank, *How Life Moves*, North Atlantic Books, 2006

T. C. McLuhan, *Touch the Earth*, Sphere Books Ltd, 1973

Lynne McTaggart, *The Intention Experiment*, Simon & Schuster, 2007

Arien Mack and Irvin Rock, *Inattentional Blindness: An Overview*, Cambridge MIT Press, 1998

Victor Megre, *Anastasia*, Ringing Cedars Press, 1996

Jan Panksepp, *Affective NeuroScience: The Foundations of Human and Animal Emotions*, Oxford University Press, 1998

Clive Ponting, *A Green History of the World*, Sinclair-Stevenson Limited, 1991

Daniel Quinn, *Ishmael*, Bantam Books, 1992

Rachel Naomi Remen, *My Grandfather's Blessings*, Riverhead Books, 2000

Don Richard Riso and Russ Hudson, *The Wisdom of the Enneagram*, Bantam, 1999

Anthony Robbins, *Giant Steps*, Fireside, 1994

Gabrielle Roth, *Maps to Ecstasy*, New World Library, 1989

—, *Sweat Your Prayers*, Jeremy P. Tarcher/Putnam, 1997

—, *Connections*, Jeremy P. Tarcher, 2004

Victor Sanchez, *Toltecs of the New Millennium*, Inner Traditions International, 1996

Anna Ancelin Schutzenberger, *The Ancestor Syndrome*, Routledge, 1998

Andrew Simms and Jo Smith, *Do Good Lives Have to Cost the Earth?*, Constable, 2008

Elisabet Sahtouris and James Lovelock, *Earthdance: Living Systems in Evolution,* iUniversity Press, 2000

Miranda Tuffnell and Chris Crickmay, *A Widening Field: Journeys in Body and Imagination*, Dance Books Ltd, 2003

Lao Tzu, *Tao Te Ching*, (trans.) Jane English, Random House, Inc. 1997

Van Gogh by Vincent, (ed.) Rachel Barnes, Bracken Books, 1990

Lyall Watson, *Gifts of Unknown Things: A True Story of Nature, Healing, and Initiation from Indonesia's 'Dancing Island'*, Inner Traditions International, 1991

Ken Wilber, *Grace and Grit*, Shambhala, 1991

Joseph Zinker, *Creative Gestalt Therapy*, Knopf Doubleday Publishing Group, 1978

Resources

We recognize that these are times of great uncertainty. We have found that we need the support of good friends and community along the way. We have also benefited a lot from the work of different organizations and methods that provide us with ongoing support and inspiration for our work, and we want to share a few of those here in a small resource directory in the hope that they will be useful and supportive for you too.

Websites

www.365act.com Encouraging daily social activism.

www.bethechange.org.uk Deep and empowering symposium on climate change.

www.carbonneutral.com Good information on carbon neutral business practice.

www.cat.org.uk Alternative energy centre for research in the UK.

www.climatecrisis.net Al Gore's film *An Inconvenient Truth*.

www.crudemovie.net *The Age of Stupid* movie's website.

www.enspiriting.com/warren.htm For Warren Ziegler's work.

www.est.org.uk Plenty of information for alternative energy ideas.

www.onehundredmonths.org Speaks for itself and it's a great invitation to act now.

www.seat61.com Flight-free travel throughout Europe.

www.theecologist.org Many inspiring articles and much info online.

www.thehungersite.com A site with the intent of ending hunger worldwide.

www.therainforestsite.com Protecting virgin rainforest with the click of a mouse.

www.traidcraft.co.uk Sustainable and fairtrade shopping for the home.

www.tree2mydoor.com Give a tree to someone you love.

Do you have dreams for the future? We're setting up a webpage that focuses on positive visions for the future for life on this planet. Can you add to it?

Go to:

www.schoolofmovementmedicine/dreamsforthefuture.php

Index of Recipes

Notes

Notes

Notes

Notes

Notes

Notes

IF YOU ARE INTERESTED IN EXPLORING THE PRACTICES
AND PHILOSOPHIES PRESENTED IN THIS BOOK
the School of Movement Medicine offers an international
programme of events and workshops, ranging from introductory
evenings, to weekend workshops, intensives, and ongoing groups.

We also offer an 18-month Apprenticeship Programme
which is followed by Professional Training for those
who wish to teach Movement Medicine.

FOR MORE INFORMATION SEE OUR WEBSITE OR CONTACT:
roland@RWEvents.co.uk · +44 (0)1803 762 255

FOR MUSIC, GUIDED MEDITATIONS AND OTHER PRODUCTS TO
SUPPORT YOUR PRACTICE: www.movementmedicineshop.com

DARE TO DANCE · DARE TO DREAM

SCHOOL OF MOVEMENT MEDICINE
www.schoolofmovementmedicine.com

Hay House Titles of Related Interest

We hope you enjoyed this Hay House book.
If you would like to receive a free catalogue featuring additional
Hay House books and products, or if you would like information
about the Hay Foundation, please contact:

Hay House UK Ltd
292B Kensal Road • London W10 5BE
Tel: (44) 20 8962 1230; Fax: (44) 20 8962 1239
www.hayhouse.co.uk

***

Published and distributed in the United States of America by:
Hay House, Inc. • PO Box 5100 • Carlsbad, CA 92018-5100
Tel: (1) 760 431 7695 or (1) 800 654 5126;
Fax: (1) 760 431 6948 or (1) 800 650 5115
www.hayhouse.com

***

Published and distributed in Australia by:
Hay House Australia Ltd • 18/36 Ralph Street • Alexandria, NSW 2015
Tel: (61) 2 9669 4299, Fax: (61) 2 9669 4144
www.hayhouse.com.au

***

Published and distributed in the Republic of South Africa by:
Hay House SA (Pty) Ltd • PO Box 990 • Witkoppen 2068
Tel/Fax: (27) 11 467 8904
www.hayhouse.co.za

***

Published and distributed in India by:
Hay House Publishers India • Muskaan Complex • Plot No.3
B-2 • Vasant Kunj • New Delhi - 110 070
Tel: (91) 11 41761620; Fax: (91) 11 41761630
www.hayhouse.co.in

***

Distributed in Canada by:
Raincoast • 9050 Shaughnessy St • Vancouver, BC V6P 6E5
Tel: (1) 604 323 7100
Fax: (1) 604 323 2600

***

Sign up via the Hay House UK website to receive the Hay House
online newsletter and stay informed about what's going on with your
favourite authors. You'll receive bimonthly announcements
about discounts and offers, special events, product highlights,
free excerpts, giveaways, and more!
www.hayhouse.co.uk

HAY HOUSE PUBLISHERS